Nancy is one of the leading experts in VSED for the end-of-life practitioner world. She is my "go to" for end-of-life options and compassionate, caring consultation. I trust her 100% and refer the students and graduates of my program to her. She is a dedicated advocate, and I'm proud to be her colleague and friend. This publication is a key new reference guide!

Deanna Cochran
RN, Founder of Certified CareDoula® Education

My mother was one of the hardy souls Nancy Simmers helped navigate the VSED passage. The warmth and skill she brought to my entire family are captured here in this book. Nancy will take your hand and walk you through the VSED process step-by-step. The chapters unfold with the information as you need to know it, and when you can assimilate it. The apt comparison to labor and birth shows that the labor of exiting the planet is as natural as the labor of being born. Very few people combine Simmers' nursing background with her deep, pragmatic knowledge of VSED. An invaluable resource.

Kathryn Trueblood
Professor, Western Washington University
Daughter of woman who used VSED to hasten her death

Nancy has had experience dealing with both the early and last stages of life. Now, Nancy uses her extensive knowledge about VSED to support people who have made this choice at the end of their life's journey. If we are healthy and tending to our elders, or if we are nearing the end of our life, each of us can learn from Nancy's wisdom and experience.

Phyllis Shacter
Author of *Choosing to Die, A Personal Story*

In her work with VSED Resources Northwest, Nancy Simmers has undoubtedly guided as many cases of VSED as anyone in the U.S. Nancy's participation in the national writing group that created the first US national VSED Clinical Guidelines brought a death doula's valuable perspective to the first guide for clinicians. Now this informative, practical guide to VSED will be a highly meaningful resource for patients and families.

Paul T. Menzel
Professor of Philosophy emeritus, Pacific Lutheran University

As a compassionate, seasoned, highly respected advocate in the right-to-die movement, Nancy brings her entire self to her craft. *VSED Support: What Friends and Family Need to Know* is both a guide and a gift for anyone navigating a chosen end-of-life, and their loved ones. Bringing practical pointers, clarity and grace, Nancy demystifies VSED and restores dignity to the bedside.

Crystal C Flores
Death Doula, The Grateful Death

Nancy is an incredibly knowledgeable and encouraging advocate and colleague for VSED. When I accepted my first VSED client, Nancy provided insightful and practical guidance at every step of the process. Her consultation empowered me to offer informed and relevant support to my client and her family. As a result, they were able to focus more of their energy on sharing precious time together, and my client died peacefully, on her terms. an important new resource for Death Doulas and the families navigating VSED.

Kate Maxim
Death Doula, Heart of the Valley End-of-Life Community

Together Nancy and I have developed our VSED death doula practice over the past 6 years. We continue to serve as board members of the non-profit we helped form in 2019, VSED Resources Northwest, a national educational resource for Voluntarily Stopping Eating and Drinking. Our collegial support of one another has certainly benefitted our own practice, and has also enhanced the advocacy for end-of-life choices throughout the Pacific Northwest and now the entire nation. Nancy's book, *VSED Support: What Friends and Family Need to Know*, is a culmination of knowledge and experience gleaned over these years. It is a welcomed resource for death doulas and the people who trust in their care.

Andrea Fenwick
Death Doula, Pathway Home Doulas
Board member, VSED Resources Northwest
Co-founder, The Last Dance Death Doula & Caregiver Collective

Nancy blends deep compassion with a scientific knowledge of the physiology of dying on one's own terms.
Dwight Moore, Ph.D.
Past Chairman, Arizona End of Life Choices

Nancy Simmers has written an exquisite guide for those interested in VSED and their families and friends. The preparation and the process of VSED is described in a very readable step-by-step format. Most importantly, there is a thread of compassion woven throughout. Nancy is the most heartful person I know, and her kindness shines through on every page.
Kathryn J. Fentress, Ph.D.
Psychologist, Author of *Playbook for Surfing the Paradigm Shift*

VSED Support

What Friends and Family Need to Know

A HELPFUL REFERENCE FOR VOLUNTARILY STOPPING EATING AND DRINKING

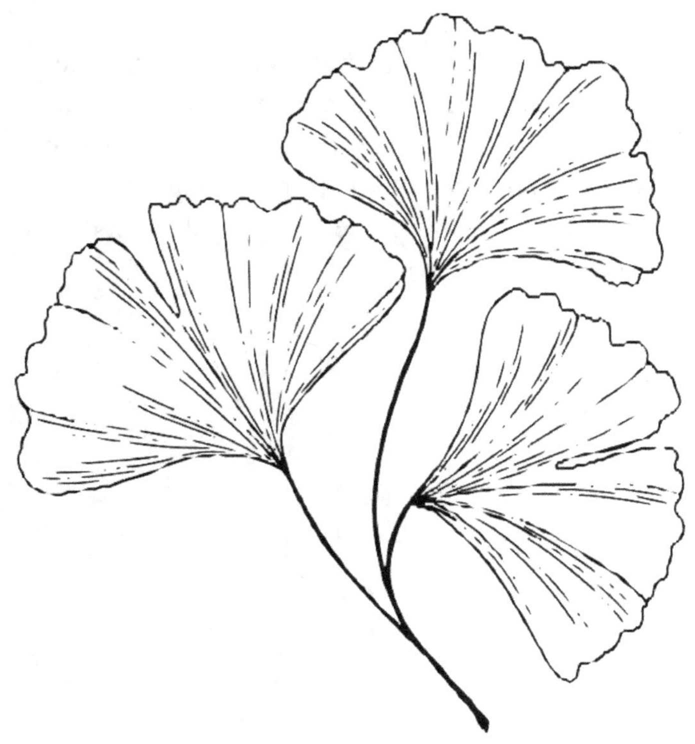

Nancy Simmers, BSN, RN, End-of-Life Doula

Printed in the USA with the help of Village Books.
Bellingham, Washington

ISBN: 9798234073464
Library of Congress Control Number: 2026912052

Second Edition

Cover design and interior design by Malia Wortman, Assistantside

Disclaimer: The information contained in this book is for educational purposes only. It is not intended as a substitute for professional medical, legal, or psychological advice. Readers should consult available and qualified professionals before making decisions regarding health care, end-of-life choices, or legal matters.

Dear Readers,

A person considering VSED for themselves, or a friend or family member invited into the circle of support, will have many questions about the preparation that has taken place and what they see and hear each day of VSED.

They may seek help in understanding the entire VSED process and the thoughtful planning that has happened.

Above all, they will wonder how best to be supportive.

This book aims to address those important questions.

Nancy Simmers, BSN, RN, End-of-Life Doula

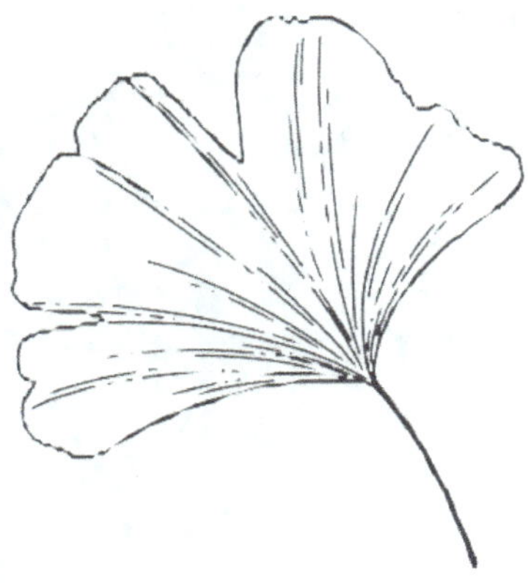

For All of Us Who Are Dying

May your death come gently toward you,
leaving you time to make your way
intentionally through the cold embrace of fear
and into the place of inner tranquility.

May death arrive to find you dying as you envisioned:
at home among your own
with every comfort and care you require.

May your leave-taking be gracious,
enabling you to hold your dignity and peace
through any awkwardness and challenge of illness.

May you see the reflection
of your life's kindness and beauty
in all the tears that fall for you.

May your heart be speechless and fulfilled
at the sight of all for which you had hoped.

~ Anonymous

GRATITUDE

This book would not have been written without the help of Diane Hullet. When I was her podcast guest on the subject of VSED in 2024, our friendship blossomed. Later, when I shared my vision of this book, the synergy that sparked between us propelled me into a writing frenzy. (Thank you, typing cat meme!) Our weekly check-ins focused on next steps to complete, which kept me in motion. Diane was generous with her time, encouraging me with suggestions, rewrites, and good humor. From the start, she called herself a "midwife for projects." She is that, and also my soul sister. Heartfelt thanks.

DEDICATION

To Frank, Jane, Sara, Carolyn, Cindy, Mike, David, Gillian, Nancy, Gloria, Pat,
William, Leticia, Linda, Geoff, and Gwen
who, in their living and dying, were the best teachers.

To my sister-colleagues who courageously formed VSED Resources Northwest
and continue to spread far and wide the news that VSED is
a legal and necessary option to end suffering at the end of life.

To the members of the Clinical Guidelines Writing Group, who invited this end-
of-life doula to participate in the writing of the first-ever, US-published VSED
Clinical Guidelines, and who continue to advocate for VSED,
both in the US and internationally.

To End of Life Washington, for advocating for VSED for those who do not
qualify to use Washington State's Death with Dignity Law.

To Phyllis Shacter and Josselyn Winslow and Trudy James,
true end-of-life pioneers and mentors.

To my colleagues in The Last Dance Collective
of Death Doulas and Caregivers.

To Andrea Fenwick, my doula partner and inspiration.

To the untold number of friends and family
who support their loved-ones' choices at the end of life.

CONTENTS

Part III. What Are the Stages of the VSED Process?

Stage 1 - Beginning of VSED

Stage 2 - Middle of VSED

Stage 3 - End of VSED

Stage 4 – Death & After-Death Considerations

Expanded Resources

Author's Reflections and Notes

About the Author

Glossary of Terms Used in the Book

The first time I met Nancy Simmers, I could tell she carried a wealth of knowledge about Voluntarily Stopping Eating and Drinking (VSED), and that a book would be the perfect way to share it widely.

Her years of experience with the process of dying in all its forms – through nursing, volunteering, and working for hospice and in palliative care – prepare her to offer guidance that is both knowledgeable and compassionate.

For many, VSED offers a way to hasten death and remain rooted in dignity. Having a measure of control over how and when one dies can bring peace of mind to those facing decline, pain, or loss of autonomy. Nancy has written this book to answer commonly asked questions and offer practical support around this decision, particularly for friends and family members who are close to the person choosing VSED.

The decision to enact VSED is not simple, and it is not for everyone. It requires organization, dedication and planning. But for some, it is a path that feels aligned with their values, their bodies, and their sense of self.

As an educator who seeks to encourage all of us to face our mortality, I believe we can learn by drawing on the wisdom of people who, like Nancy, have walked alongside the dying, listened without judgment, and witnessed the deeply personal choices that help someone face death on their own terms.

Whatever your circumstances – whether you yourself are considering VSED, or whether you are supporting another – I wish you the courage to face what's ahead and the grace to meet it fully.

Diane Hullet
End-of-Life Educator, Doula
and Host of the *Best Life Best Death Podcast*

Introduction

As this generation of Boomers rolls into elderhood, they are redefining and reclaiming personal choice. In the 1960s they insisted birth was a natural experience, not a medical one. Now this same generation wants choice at the end of life. Unlike the generation who raised them, Boomers are more willing to talk about death and dying. They are engaged in improving all aspects of aging within their local communities – housing, transportation, medical care, access to adequate food and social interaction. They are in the forefront of local, state and national organizations advocating for end-of-life choices.

Our media predicts Baby Boomers (born between 1945 and 1964) will constitute a "Silver Tsunami" facing serious illnesses and deaths in their later years. Current census shows that by 2030, there will be more people over 65 than under 18, a historic first for the United States. It's clear that our healthcare system won't be able to handle this impact, and there won't be enough unpaid caregivers – family and friends – for those in advanced illness.

This has led to a growing awareness of the role of death doulas or end-of-life guides. These professionals accompany individuals one-on-one as they navigate the challenges of aging, changes in physical and mental abilities, and the culmination of a chronic illness or a new health crisis. They also help people deal with an overwhelmed healthcare system, resistance to discuss end-of-life choices from family members and healthcare professionals, and the grief of losing lifelong friends and family members.

Many people want to reclaim their power and ability to prepare for the very natural process of saying goodbye to the body, sometimes by even choosing how and when to end their suffering and hasten death.

If your family member or friend has chosen to die via VSED, it can be hard to watch them refuse what has always sustained them – drink and food, which in every culture symbolizes care, hospitality, nurturance and love. The body literally fades in stature, energy, ability, and capacity. Death comes in a matter of days.

Our human impulse is to personalize what we see another person experience – to imagine ourselves in that situation. We can become frightened and pull away from what we're witnessing unless we understand what we are seeing and hearing and why this happens.

This book will help you understand your loved one's preparation for VSED so you can support them compassionately. By offering support, you honor their choice to end life in a way that reflects their physical, emotional, and spiritual needs.

This book is a heartfelt tribute to the family and friends who surround a loved one during their final days. It also offers valuable insights and suggestions for self-care and soul-care, empowering readers to step forward and provide support as the VSED process unfolds.

Witnessing the VSED process is a precious opportunity to be with another human being as they transition from an embodied person to a spiritual presence. May this book be a guide for your role as a caring companion.

Why This Book about VSED?

♥ The Heart of the Matter

This book strives to answer questions so that family members and friends who are helping can be better informed, less fearful, more understanding of their own needs and reactions, and more tolerant of what they see and hear from one another and the Individual whose death-plan brings them together.

VSED Support is written mainly for the family and friends of a person who has made the decision to hasten their death through voluntarily stopping eating and drinking, or VSED (pronounced "vee-said"). Throughout these pages, that person will be respectfully referred to as the Individual (with a capital I).

Although the Individual who chooses VSED has carefully prepared for this life-changing event, family members and friends, upon learning of this choice, may find themselves perplexed, even overwhelmed, by what has been planned, by what lies ahead and by how best to be of help.

Those in the support role may have many questions which cannot be answered by the dying Individual because of urgency of time, difficulty in speaking caused by a disease process, or a myriad of other human reasons, including fatigue, embarrassment, shame, doubt, separation, estrangement and pain. This publication will serve as a reference for all involved.

When family and friends are included in the sacred circle of support for this death-journey, they may have additional questions about what they are seeing, hearing, and witnessing on a daily basis. This guidebook aims to answer those questions.

Because they may struggle with their Individual's decision to VSED, this material serves as a neutral, straight-forward resource to provide understanding about the realities of VSED, even if the reader never fully agrees with the decision and continues to feel deep grief about the choice made.

Death, like birth, can be complicated because of the human interactions. Feelings and fears, assumptions and past experiences add to the complexities. This book does not assume that the Individual who has chosen to undertake VSED is unconditionally beloved by the friends and family members in their support circle. Nor does it assume that all friends and family members are angelic, compassionate people of service. We are human, and death can bring out the best in us as well as the imperfect, unskilled aspects of our lives. Communication and self-care are paramount.

Because of their knowledge, experience and communication, the presence of a death doula can have a profound effect on every aspect of VSED and everyone involved. This publication encourages incorporating the services of a death doula and describes how a death doula facilitates each stage of VSED, from beginning to end, and afterwards.

Please note: This book does not include information regarding the ways in which various diseases may affect the VSED process. Those details are beyond the scope and purpose of this book.

Also please note: Although this book is intended as a helpful overview of the preparation for and stages of the VSED process, it is not a manual for managing a VSED experience. More specific and detailed information about preparing for and managing a VSED process can be found in the resources listed in the Appendices and in *The VSED Manual for Death Doulas*, also written by Nancy Simmers and due to be published in Spring 2026.

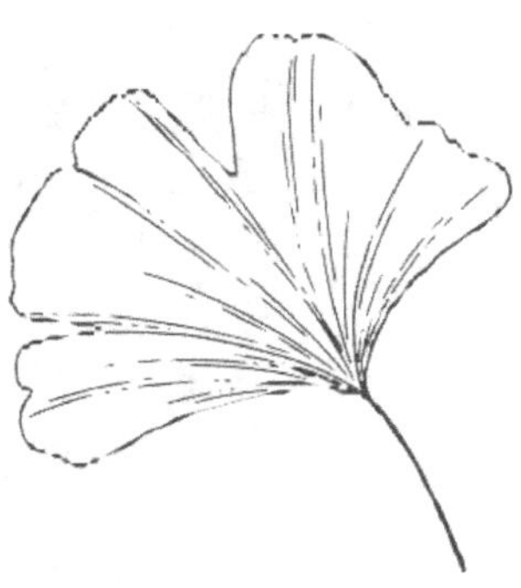

How Can This Book Best Be Used?

- The intention of this book is to answer potentially complex or controversial topics in a neutral way, with clearly-stated facts and a tone of support, compassion, and respect.
- The book is divided into four sections:

  Part I. What is VSED?

  Part II. How Does Someone Prepare for VSED?

  Part III. What Are the Stages of the VSED Process?

  Part IV. Expanded Resources
- Each section is organized around commonly asked questions under those topics.
- The answers, in bullet point format, are easy to read. Explanations aim to give information in a compact format.
- Many words and phrases are explained in more detail in the glossary at the end on page 88.
- In the section "What Are the Stages of the VSED Process?" some material is repeated when it fits into more than one stage, in order to save the reader time in cross-referencing.
- For clarity, the person using VSED is referred to as the "Individual," and support-circle members are referred to as "friends or family members."

What's Most Important to Know about VSED?

❤ The Heart of the Matter

VSED is a legal choice made by an Individual with the mental ability to choose it. VSED is a personal choice, an expression of one's own personal autonomy. It is legal in all 50 U.S. states, and it has ancient roots in humanity's experience of dying.

- The Individual choosing this way to hasten their death needs personal care and attention, as well as expressions of love and support.

- The circle of support around the Individual needs knowledge of this complex, multi-day process.

- Every death is unique to the Individual who is dying; each VSED experience is unique.

- Thorough preparation must be completed before starting VSED for the care and comfort of the Individual.

- VSED is best done with hospice service which will provide medication, supervision, education, and support.

- Death via VSED happens when organs can no longer function from lack of water and energy.

- Hiring caregivers is encouraged so that family members and friends can lovingly attend to their Individual, as well as tend to their own needs for rest, food, sleep, and support.

- The average VSED is 5-10 days, and occasionally longer.

Part I.

What Is VSED?

Q: What is the definition of VSED?

- VSED is an acronym for Voluntarily Stopping Eating and Drinking, pronounced, "Vee-said."
- It is a completely voluntary process, undertaken by an Individual who has decision-making capacity.
- VSED is freely chosen, a legally protected expression of personal autonomy.
- It is a deliberate choice to end one's life by refusing all food and water, which results in the physiological process of dehydration. It
- requires careful planning and engagement of outside support, including a medical team, caregivers, death doula, and hospice.

Q: Is VSED legal?

- Yes.
- Everyone has the right to refuse nourishment and medical treatment if they have the capacity to make a voluntary and informed choice to do so.

Q: Is VSED a new thing?

- Not really. Dying by not eating or drinking has happened for eons; but the term "VSED" may be relatively new.
- There is no way of knowing how many people choose to end their life in this manner because it is not recorded on death certificates. No VSED statistics are mandated by any US state.
- Our death-phobic society does not talk easily about end-of-life options and decisions.
- Physicians are educated to promote life-saving practices and treatments and may be hesitant to talk about options such as VSED. It is possible that they may do so only if their patients introduce the topic.
- National VSED Clinical Guidelines did not exist in the US to guide physician management of VSED until they were published in 2023. (See Heart of the Matter on page 33 and also Appendix VI for these guidelines.)

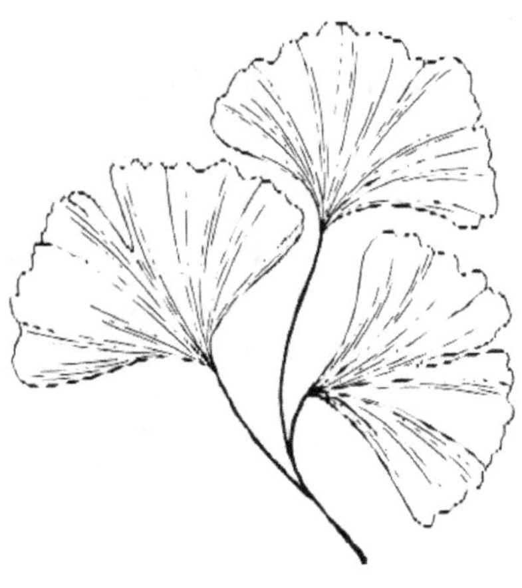

Q: Is VSED suicide?

- No.
- A person who commits suicide no longer wants to live and often acts impulsively or in secret.
- An Individual who chooses to use VSED would prefer to live, but without suffering or unacceptable deterioration.
- The consequences of suicide and sudden death are often traumatic for friends and family.
- The anticipatory grief of VSED is different, with time and shared knowledge changing the experience of grief.
- VSED must be thoughtfully planned with medical consultation and the support of friends and/or family.
- The VSED process may be private, but is not completed in secret, as medical, caregiving, and family support are critically important.

Q: Why is VSED not suicide?

- VSED is freely chosen, a legally guaranteed expression of personal autonomy.
- It is made by an Individual with decisional capacity.
- It requires careful planning and engagement of outside support, including caregivers and hospice.
- It is neither violent nor impulsively done.

Q: Why does an individual choose VSED?

- An Individual might experience suffering that is unremitting, and that is not eased with comfort care interventions, such as palliative care.
- They might be in the midst of a prolonged dying that they find intolerable.
- They may have a terminal illness and face a future of deterioration or suffering that they find unacceptable.
- They might be ineligible for Medical Aid in Dying (MAID) or live in a state that does not have a law allowing MAID.

Q: What is decisional capacity?

The parts of decision-making capacity are an understanding of:
- the underlying diagnosis and prognosis with VSED;
- the necessary preparation for and process of VSED;
- the potential physical challenges and how they can be managed;
- demonstrated consistency, both verbally or in writing, over time, in choosing to pursue VSED;
- the social and emotional challenges that may accompany VSED.

Q: What is the physical process of VSED?

- Every cell of the body contains water.
- Without water the body's organ systems begin to fail.
- Without food the body's energy stores are depleted.
- Circulation is shunted to the body core, the brain-heart-lungs.
- Coma and organ failure lead to death.

Q: How long does it take to complete VSED?

- Varies from 5-15 days.
- Average time is 5-10 days.

Q: How does a medical professional, such as a family practice doctor, primary care physician, or palliative care physician, support an Individual choosing VSED?

- Listens with respect and openness as the Individual talks about their decision.
- Acknowledges the Individual's right of personal autonomy.
- Refers to another provider if unable to support the Individual.
- Reviews the VSED process with the Individual to help them understand the Beginning, Middle, and End stages of the process.
- Makes a referral to hospice. If needed, assists Individual in finding a supportive hospice service.
- Reviews the Individual's Advance Directives and POLST for completeness, including possibly, a directive about what to do if certain difficult things happen specific to the VSED process after the person has lost capacity.
- Writes prescription, if needed, for medications to be used before admission to hospice.
- Counsels about how and when to stop current medication regimen.
- Discusses the importance of 24-hour-caregiving for safety.
- Supports the family by being available to them and answering questions.
- Makes a home visit if at all possible.
- Signs the death certificate, if appropriate.
- Makes sure family is aware of community bereavement support.

Q: What medication is available and sometimes used during VSED?

- Morphine (liquid form) – for difficulty breathing, pain
- Lorazepam (liquid form) – for anxiety
- Haloperidol (liquid form) – if needed for delirium
- Fentanyl (patch) – if needed for pain
- Scopolamine (patch) – if needed for nausea or to dry secretions

Q: Is VSED reversible?

- Yes. In the first few days, before an Individual becomes unconscious, the process can be stopped with the ingestion of fluids.

Q: What information is recorded on the death certificate?

- The Individual's underlying disease process is usually recorded as the cause of death.
- Sometimes the term "dehydration" or "organ failure" is recorded, and sometimes the term "inanition." The term "inanition" means exhaustion caused by lack of nutrition.

Q: Does death by VSED void life insurance policies?

- No. This is not a consideration because VSED is not suicide.

Q: What physical discomforts can be experienced and what can be done to help?

- **Hunger**: May be experienced during the first 1-2 days. This can be helped by decreasing calories prior to start date.

- **Intestinal cramping**: May be experienced as the normal flow of digested food through the intestines is slowed due to medication and lack of activity. Constipation can be prevented by decreasing food intake a few days before starting VSED and by using an enema the day before the start date of VSED.

- **Dry mouth and throat**: Caused by not drinking fluids. Use of a cool air vaporizer, plus frequent mouth care and applying moisturizer to the face and lips is helpful.

- **Nausea**: May be experienced in the first 1-2 days. Medication and acupuncture are used to alleviate these symptoms.

- **Confusion**: Can occur as the dehydration process continues. Medication, personal care, and attentive care are used to support the Individual.

- **Anxiety**: Can accompany the confusion. Medication, distraction, personal care and attentive care are used to calm and guide the Individual.

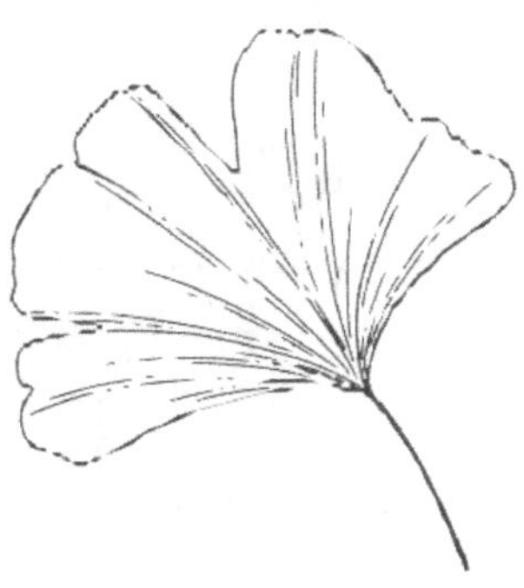

A death doula is a non-medical companion who provides emotional, practical, and logistical support through the dying process. They help coordinate care, facilitate important conversations, and oversee the many details that arise at the end of life. Their presence offers steady guidance and reassurance during one of life's biggest transitions, and they can play a key role in supporting Individuals and their caregivers through the process of VSED.

Q: What role can a death doula have with VSED?

- Explains the VSED process in detail, answers questions throughout the VSED experience.
- Talks with Individual and family regarding plans and preferences for rituals before, during and after, and how these can impact the experience for the entire family.
- Recommends ways to establish markers to better determine a start date, as well as how to track markers over time prior to start date.
- Suggests necessary legal documents that need to be completed and how to access them.
- Makes certain a referral to hospice is made and received.
- Serves as part of the palliative care team of support, coordinating with hospice staff.
- Helps find VSED-experienced caregivers as well as other supportive community resources, such as Threshold Singers, caregiving supply sources, funeral homes, etc.
- Coordinates with Individual's healthcare professional, hospice staff, caregivers, family members and friends.
- Offers ideas for body disposition, memorial tributes, and composing obituary and eulogy.
- Once the VSED process begins, is in attendance daily to assess the VSED process, encourage the patient, support the family and caregivers.

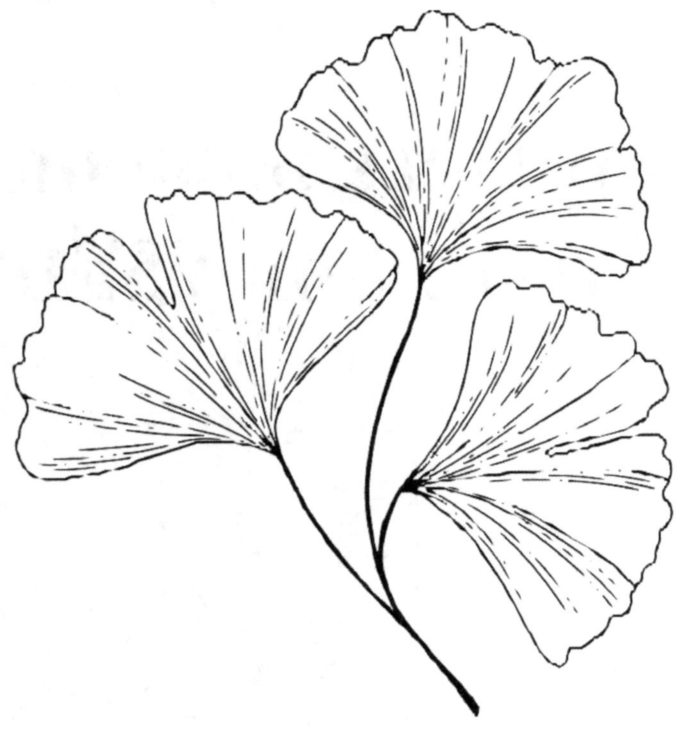

Part II.

How Does Someone Prepare For VSED?

> ♥ The Heart of the Matter
>
> VSED can offer someone who is suffering a much sought-after "exit ramp." However, VSED requires careful planning, clear thinking, and determination.

Q: How can family members and friends support the Individual who chooses VSED?

- Be fully present and attentive, curious and open, willing to be of service.
- Simultaneously, be aware of one's own limitations and boundaries.
- Be responsible for one own's self-care: regular meals, sleep, breaks, time alone, outside activities.
- Be willing to listen if the Individual wishes to speak about their choice to VSED.
- Listen if the Individual discusses steps for planning their VSED.
- Ask specifically what they would like you to do to show your support at this time.

Q: What if someone declines to be part of the support circle?

- The decision to prematurely end one's life by VSED is a deeply personal, moral and ethical decision.
- As with all significant life-cycle decisions, this choice may be the opposite of what others would choose.
- If a friend or family member is <u>unable</u> to be part of the support circle, saying so early on is recommended. Sharing this decision with the person coordinating the VSED process, usually a doula or family member, will clarify roles and help with understanding.
- If one chooses to disengage from the VSED support circle itself, there may be other ways of showing support to the Individual's support circle, such as errands, household help, rides, etc.

Q: What if someone disagrees with the idea of VSED?

- People going through the VSED process need total love and support.
- If one has concerns about the Individual's choice, speak about them with another trusted person who can listen to you with neutrality. The death doula may be someone with whom to talk, also the hospice social worker or chaplain, or a representative of your faith-based community.
- Keep in mind that your support of the dying Individual in no way commits you to choose VSED for yourself.
- Remember that VSED is a legal choice and in no way legally incriminates you.
- If more than one family member or friend questions the decision, a family mediator may be helpful.
- If unable to support the Individual who has chosen VSED, consider supporting additional family members who are present and likely need a variety of help.
- Ultimately, if no resolution can be found for one's dilemma and objection, it may be best to withdraw from the situation.

Q: What legal documents might be necessary in preparing for a VSED death?

- **Will and/or estate planning documents** – if appropriate and necessary.
- **Durable Power of Attorney for Healthcare (DPOA-HC)** – the person who will make your medical decisions if you are unable.
- **VSED Advance Directive** This document instructs the health care agent or legal decision-maker about how to act on their behalf, ensuring one's wishes for VSED are carried out. (https://www.washingtonlawhelp.org/resource/vsed-directive)
- **Video of Individual recording why they wish to use VSED** – this can be recorded on a cell phone and transferred to any device as part of the VSED Advance Directive.
- **Hold Harmless document** – (optional) protects hired caregivers and support persons during the VSED process, and legally ends with the death of the Individual.
- **Durable Power of Attorney for Finances (DPOA-F)** – the person who will manage your finances if you are unable.
- **Release of Information Form** – allows personal information to be shared between Individual's physician, hospice, death doula and caregivers, facilitating them working together as a team.

Q: How can 2 videos help in preparation?

- Two distinct videos can be helpful:
  - The Individual can make a video explaining their thinking about this decision. This video is made to explain to others.
  - The Individual can make a brief video in which they are speaking to their future self. This video is made to share with themselves and can be shown to the Individual at any point of confusion during the VSED process.

Q: How does a medical professional support an Individual choosing VSED?

- Listens with respect and openness as the Individual talks about their decision.
- Acknowledges the Individual's right of personal autonomy.
- Refers to another provider if unable to support the Individual.
- Reviews the VSED process with the Individual to help them understand the Beginning, Middle, and End stages of the process.
- Makes a referral to hospice. If needed, assists Individual in finding a supportive hospice service.
- Reviews the Advance Directives and POLST/MOLST for completeness and understanding.
- Writes prescription, if needed, for medications to be used before admission to hospice.
- Counsels about how and when to stop current medication regimen.
- Discusses the importance of 24-hour-caregiving for safety.
- Supports the family by being available to them.
- Makes a home visit if at all possible.
- Signs the death certificate, if needed.
- Makes sure family is aware of community bereavement support.

Q: How is a death doula helpful with preparation for VSED?

- The death doula explains the VSED process in detail, and answers questions throughout the VSED experience.
- Serves as part of the palliative care team of support, coordinating with hospice staff.
- Counsels about how to establish markers for the start date, as well as how to track markers over time.
- Helps family find VSED-experienced caregivers as well as other supportive community resources, such as Threshold Singers or sources for medical equipment.
- Coordinates with Individual's healthcare professional, hospice staff, caregivers, family members and friends.
- Talks with the Individual and family regarding plans and preferences for body disposition, rituals, memorial tributes as well as educating them about the variety of options that are available.
- Available to help family compose obituary and eulogy.
- Helps organize and facilitate a gathering, ceremony or ritual to mark the beginning of VSED.

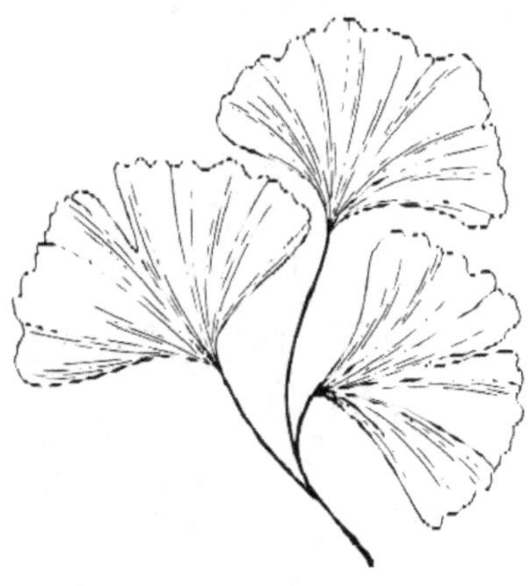

Q: What role does a death doula play once VSED is underway?

- Visits daily to assess the VSED process, encourage the patient, support the family and caregivers.
- Serves as the consistent "point person" or hub for all communication and any plan changes.
- Encourages family members to eat and sleep regularly for their own self-care.
- Is available to provide anticipatory grief care to family and caregivers.
- Explains to family and caregivers what changes they may see in the preceding day, giving anticipatory guidance.
- Serves as gate-keeper if necessary for the Individual using VSED regarding who is welcomed into the circle of support.
- After the death, can gently remind friends and family of the Individual's preferences for after-death care and help coordinate that taking place.
- Remains in touch with family representative for a pre-determined period of time, to help assess their individual expression of bereavement and to help process the VSED experience from their perspective.
- Meets with caregivers, following the death, to review their perceptions of the VSED experience and to help process any challenging aspects of the entire experience or feedback for the family.

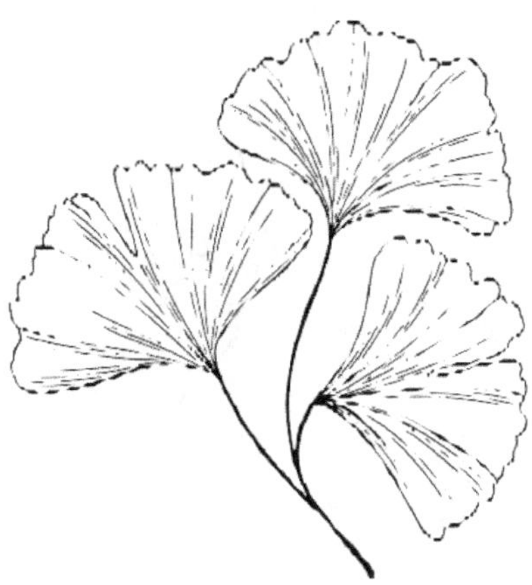

Q: What role does hospice play in VSED?

- Hospice provides palliative care service, comfort care, for people who have a terminal diagnosis and a prognosis with an expected life span of less than six months.
- Referrals for hospice care are made by a clinician (MD, Physician Assistant, Nurse Practitioner) who provides Individual's diagnosis and medical records.
- A hospice care team is usually comprised of a registered nurse (RN), social worker, chaplain and bath aide, and the team is overseen by a Hospice Medical Director.
- Hospice services can be delivered in the home, a residential facility, a care center or dementia care facility.
- Consultation by hospice is available on a 24/7 basis and RN visits are determined by need.
- An intake interview will determine eligibility for hospice services as well as schedule of services.
- Hospice services are usually covered by Medicaid, but not usually by long-term insurance.
- Hospice services do not include 24/7 caregiving.

Q: What's the difference between a death doula and a hospice social worker? Are both needed?

- Both are members of an individual's palliative care team, coordinating support and education for the individual and their family.
- The death doula, employed by the individual, works with one case at a time during VSED, providing in-depth education and continuous support.
- The hospice social worker, part of the palliative team once hospice involvement occurs, has a caseload, limiting time and contact.
- Together, they make a powerful team of support for the family, each providing comprehensive service.

Q: What are the considerations when hiring personal caregivers?

- Someone needs to be with the Individual using VSED at all times, to monitor them for safety and provide needed caregiving.
- It is optimal to hire caregivers who are experienced with VSED. A death doula can help make this referral to VSED-experienced caregivers.
- Hired caregivers help family members maintain a daily schedule of sleep, food, and rest, enabling them to be present and meaningful family members.
- Caregiving by hired workers allows family members to pace their support and process their grief.
- It is best to hire caregivers who can commit to a two-week schedule, to provide needed consistency for patient and family.
- Two weeks of 24/7 caregiving is a financial burden for many families, likely totaling $10-14,000.
- Medicare and Medicaid and Long-Term Care Insurance do not cover these expenses.

Q: Where can an Individual best carry out VSED?

- People are usually most comfortable in their own homes.
- Hospices with home-based programs are usually available.
- Some facilities do not allow VSED on their premises.
- If living in a care facility, best to check with administration and review the facility policies.
- Residential facilities usually allow VSED.

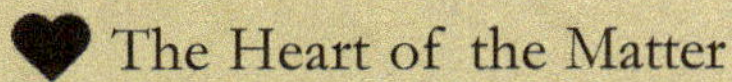 The Heart of the Matter

Preparing for personal care in advance can reduce anxiety and strengthen the bond between the person choosing VSED and their caregivers. Simple steps like trying out mouth care products or practicing how to handle food requests can make sure the support feels gentle, respectful, and in line with the Individual's wishes. Familiarity can bring comfort and confidence, but it's important to remember that preferences can change over time during the VSED process.

Q: What aspects of personal care are best discussed and practiced before the start of VSED?

- Teach and practice oral care, including use of mouth swabs, small soft tooth brush, lip balm, mouth moisturizing, etc.
- Practicing ahead of the start of VSED provides information, comfort and reassurance.
- The death doula will help write out a short script to use and practice should the Individual request fluids or food during the VSED experience.
- The death doula will also have the Individual practice with the short video (shown via cell phone), should it be needed, to remind the Individual, in their own voice, why they have chosen VSED.

Use the following topics as a starting point to discuss personal care:

- **Bathing and toileting** – Who is Individual comfortable with providing this care?
- **Touch** – What is considered comforting, what is not?
- **Smell** – What aromas are pleasing and which are not?
- **Sounds** – What kind of music is enjoyed? Prefer quiet?
- **Vision** – What would Individual enjoy looking at? (photo albums, family pictures, movies)
- **Visitors** – Who, when, and for how long? (know that this can change)
- **Private time** – Anticipate that Individual may want private time with certain individuals. Helpful to identify them ahead of time.
- **Gatekeeping** – Identify any person who is not welcome to be in Individual's presence, and identify who will notify this person. Remain aware that these preferences may change.

Q. Are there cultural aspects of death and dying that need to be observed and honored?

- The support circle might help engage the individual in acknowledging cultural practices that are meaningful in their life.
- Including current cultural practices into the planning of VSED and after-death can be a tremendous source of comfort and reassurance.
- Individuals often reflect on any cultural beliefs, ceremonies, or observances that were important in their family of origin.
- These cultural practices can be the source of meaningful conversations, and they may lead to significant inclusions in the obituary, eulogy, and after-death care and disposition.

Q. Are there religious and spiritual traditions that need to be observed and honored?

- If Individual is currently a member of a faith community, they may wish for other members of that community to be included in the support circle and may be valuable resources for additional support before and after death.
- Individuals often reflect on whatever faith tradition was practiced by their family of origin. This is often a significant topic as they review their life.
- These religious/spiritual practices can be the source of meaningful conversations and legacy work.
- These religious/spiritual practices can also add significant inclusions in the obituary, eulogy, and after-death care and disposition.

Q: What after-death care options need to be discussed and chosen?

- Plans for final arrangements for the body are best made prior to the start of VSED.
- Your death doula or hospice staff can help provide a list of funeral homes in the geographical area and discuss other options.
- If a home funeral is desired, it is important to know that such practices are legal in all 50 U.S. states. Families have the right to care for their deceased loved ones at home, including bathing, dressing, holding vigils, and conducting ceremonies. Every state recognizes the next-of-kin's custody and control of the body, allowing for home-based after-death care.
- Your doula can help with resources for body disposition choices:
  - Traditional burial with embalming or no embalming
  - Cremation, both direct and through a funeral home
  - Alkaline Hydrolysis (AH, aquamation, water cremation)
  - Green burial
  - Natural Organic Reduction (NOR, terramation, human composting)
  - Body Donation

Q: What might a support person see and hear while their Individual plans their VSED?

- Expressions of being determined, resolute, sure of decision to VSED.
- Expressions of doubt, vacillation and questioning of the VSED decision.
- Expressions of anxiety and overwhelm with all the other decisions that need to be made.
- Concern about the reactions of friends or family to the VSED decision.

Q: What can a support person do as planning is underway?

- Listen carefully with attention and reflect back what the Individual is saying.
- Acknowledge to the Individual that planning is extensive but doable.
- State one's willingness to help and ask what would be helpful.
- Be frank about what you are willing to do and what you cannot comfortably do.
- Consult the death doula if questions arise.
- Find amusement and joy! Laughter goes a long way!
- Write things down for oneself and for Individual who is planning.
- Take a break, eat something, rest – and encourage Individual to do so too.

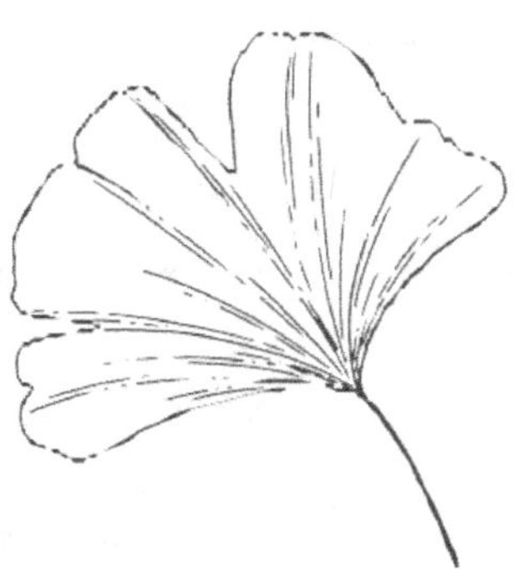

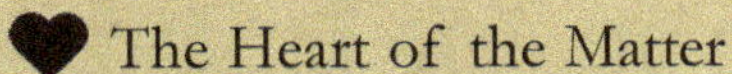 The Heart of the Matter

A death doula, together with family members, can help plan a gathering to mark the beginning of VSED. This could be a ceremony, ritual, or celebration that acknowledges the start of a person's final journey. Such a celebration, whether formal or informal, honors the individual and creates a sense of shared intention, unity and support for all who are involved.

Q: Are there helpful ways to mark and acknowledge the start of a VSED experience?

- Creating a gathering for family, friends, caregivers, and everyone who will be involved during the days of the VSED is a powerful way to meet one another and experience being a united support circle.

- A beginning ceremony is a way of setting a shared intention of caring for, loving and honoring the Individual.
  - An informal way that honors the Individual, their choice, their final journey.
  - An opportunity to share words of love and encouragement with one another.
  - A time to share family pictures, poetry, family stories, and memories.
  - A meaningful way to honor the Individual, their life and legacy.

- Sometimes we understand with our "heads," but our "souls" take time to catch up. A ceremony – whatever that means to this Individual and this support group – can help integrate head and heart.

The Similarities of Labor and Delivery to VSED

Q: What are the ways in which these two ends of the life spectrum are similar?

- Both are physical acts, spiritual/mystical experiences, and events with cultural and family significance.
- Both involve the unknown, new experiences, learning for everyone involved.
- Both are transforming for everyone involved.
- Both involve risk, pain, courage, trust of the body and the process.
- Both require physical and emotional labor; persisting through the present situation being experienced in order to transform.
- Both involve the process of letting go, of release, of surrender.
- Both can be divided into distinct physical stages for better understanding.
- Both need comfort, support, and acknowledgement.
- Both benefit from experienced, compassionate witnesses who understand what's happening.

VSED Stage 1 - Similar to early labor for birth, with anticipation, excitement, readiness, and the need for distraction to help pass the time. At this stage everything is in place for the VSED to begin and hospice usually becomes involved at this time. Symptoms of anxiety, restlessness, and shortness of breath might be experienced. Celebrations and goodbyes can happen while the Individual is conscious, or perhaps these have taken place earlier. In addition, the Individual might reconsider the decision or choose to stop the whole process. (In this, VSED differs from birth!)

VSED Stage 2 - Similar to active labor, with increased discomfort, exhaustion, anticipatory fear, and need for comfort and encouragement. This is the most difficult stage. During Stage 2, thirst increases, some delusion may occur, as well as the loss of capacity and potential agitation. The Individual will remain in bed due to weakness, and symptom management is important and essential. This is the point where one must move forward through the process.

VSED Stage 3 - Similar to the transition phase of labor, this is the pause before pushing, before delivery. It is a period of waiting, anticipation, sacred attentiveness, and quiet vigil. In this stage, the body is actively dying and the organ systems are failing. The Individual will be in and out of consciousness the majority of the time and may lapse into a coma. Ongoing holistic care and comfort measures for symptoms will be important. The death doula and caregivers will deepen their attentiveness to those who are losing the loved one, and plans for death and after-death care will be finalized.

VSED Stage 4 - Similar to the fourth stage of labor, birth, in that this is the stage of transformation. At the stage of death and after death, the physical transformation is complete, yet the mental, emotional and spiritual transitions continue to evolve. This is the final stage. Now will be the time to carry out planned and requested practices and to prepare for the body to leave the location of where it has lived and labored.

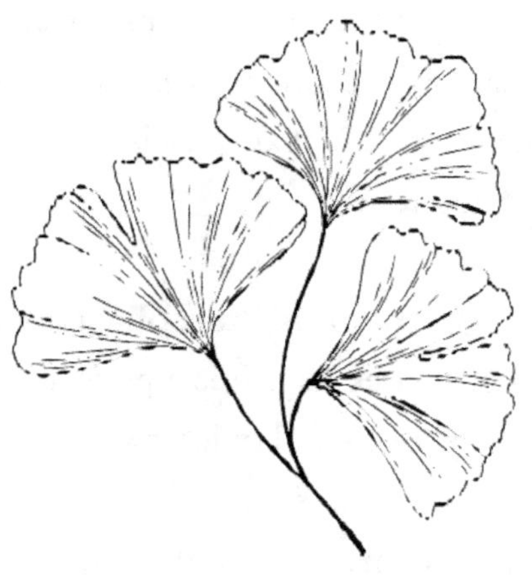

Part III.

What are the Stages of the VSED Process?

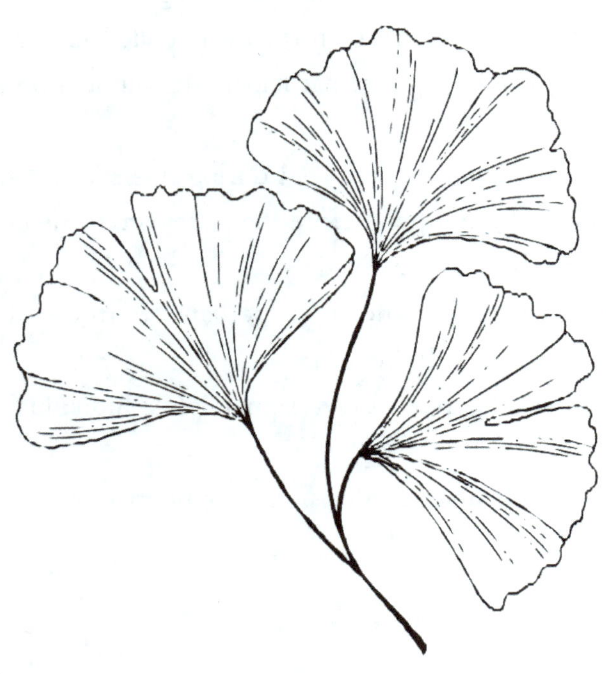

Stage 1 – Beginning of VSED

Days 1 through 3 (approximately)

Q: What are the characteristics of Stage 1 of VSED?

- Everything is in place for the VSED to begin.
- There may be an informal or formal acknowledgement of the beginning. If you can, please participate. It will help both you and the Individual.
- Hospice usually becomes involved during this stage. As noted earlier, hospice should be notified before the start date to determine the date when they can become involved.
- Symptoms of anxiety, restlessness, perhaps shortness of breath may be experienced by the Individual.
- Conversations and goodbyes can happen while Individual is still conscious.
- Possible reconsideration of decision or option to stop process may happen.

Q: What might the support person observe and hear in Stage 1?

- It may appear that nothing has changed . . . except the Individual does not eat or drink.
- Individual can engage in normal activities, except eating/drinking, for the first 24-48 hours.
- Individual may be helpfully distracted by listening to music, a conversation, visit from favorite dogs or kitties, being read aloud to, or other favorite activities.
- Individual may choose to continue to nap and sleep in their own bed or move to hospital bed in order to acclimate to it.
- Unless there are safety concerns or physical limitations, a regular bathroom toilet and shower can be used.

Q: What might the support person feel emotionally during this stage?

- Relief that preparation has come to an end and VSED has actually started.
- Concern, even anxiety, about what is to come and how long this will last.
- Conflicting emotions such as anticipatory grief and gratitude for this time together.
- Caught between desire to say something profound or meaningful and also a desire to lighten things up and distract.
- Complex and mixed emotions.

Q: What can the support person do for their own self-care and soul-care?

- Take breaks, maintain sleep routine/habits, continue to eat and drink regularly.
- Keep in mind that you are not doing the VSED – eat and drink!
- Okay to find amusement in things – death jokes or a macabre sense of humor are often okay.
- Talk with someone other than the Individual about what is being experienced and felt.
- Be creative – draw, write, create a melody and song, take pictures.
- Get outside – go for a walk or run, sit in a favorite spot.

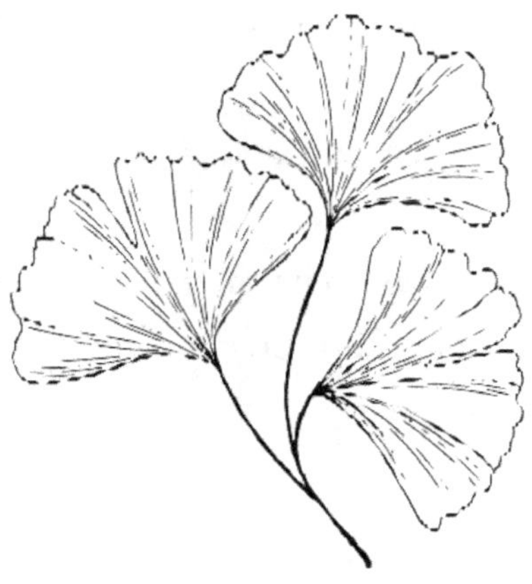

Q: What can a support person do to be helpful during this time?

- Follow the VSED-Individual's lead.
- Be a supportive presence – ask how to be helpful, or just pitch in where you know help will be accepted.
- Acknowledge the Individual for the careful and thoughtful preparation they have done.
- Help Individual establish a daily routine that does not include eating or drinking.
- Ask about preferences regarding social time, quiet time, light, music, etc. as this is respectful and acknowledging of an Individual's autonomy and control.
- Help distract and fill time with conversation, reading aloud, watching TV or movies, singing, playing cards, looking through pictures, working together on a puzzle.
- Pay attention to any subtle changes in the Individual's balance and energy level, as fatigue and loss of balance are safety factors.
- It's okay to mention to the Individual any observed changes; and it is important to share these observations with doula, caregivers, or other team members.
- Share words of encouragement and love.
- Greet Individual when arriving and leaving their presence; say when you'll return.
- Pass onto caregiver/doula any complaints of nausea, cramping, pain, or discomfort the Individual experiences.
- Remember to not bring coffee cups or water bottles into the Individual's room.
- Eat and drink away from the Individual's room and use a breath mint after eating so there are no lingering smells of food.

Q: What physical discomforts can an Individual experience with VSED and what can be done to help?

- **Hunger**: May be experienced during the first 1-2 days. This can be helped by decreasing calories prior to start date.
- **Intestinal cramping**: May be experienced as the normal flow of digested food through the intestines is slowed due to medication and lack of activity. Constipation can be prevented by decreasing food intake a few days before starting VSED and by using an enema the day before the start date of VSED.
- **Dry mouth and throat**: Caused by not drinking fluids. Use of a cool air vaporizer, plus frequent mouth care and applying moisturizer to the face and lips is helpful.
- **Nausea**: May be experienced in the first 1-2 days. Medication and acupuncture are used to alleviate these symptoms.
- **Confusion**: Can occur as the dehydration process continues. Medication, personal care, and attentive care are used to support the Individual.
- **Anxiety**: Can accompany the confusion. Medication, distraction, personal care and attentive care are used to calm and guide the Individual.

Q: What medication is used during this stage of VSED?

- **Morphine** (liquid) – for difficulty breathing, pain
- **Lorazepam** (liquid) – for anxiety
- **Haloperidol** (liquid) – if needed for delirium

Q: What holistic methods can be helpful with VSED?

- Acupuncture or acupressure
- Massage to feet, hand, face, back
- Heating pad or frozen packs
- Aromatherapy – use a diffuser, or put essential oil on a cotton ball, or use scented candle
- Healing Touch, Reiki, energy work
- Hypnosis – can be helpful for anxiety, discomfort, even nausea

Q: What is the role of the death doula during Stage 1?

- Available on a 24/7 basis to the Individual, support circle and caregivers.
- Is the consistent "point individual" as a hub for navigating communication and any changes.
- Visits daily to assess the VSED process, encourage the patient, support the family and caregivers.
- Continues to coordinate with hospice staff.
- Reviews caretaker notes each day as well as hospice nurse notes & instructions.
- Encourages family members to eat and sleep regularly for their own self-care.
- Is available to give anticipatory grief care to family and caregivers.
- Explains to family and caregivers what changes they currently notice and what they may see in the succeeding day, giving anticipatory guidance.
- Serves as gate-keeper if necessary for the Individual using VSED.
- Available to deal with the unexpected.

Stage 2 – Middle of VSED

Days 4 – 6 (approximately)

♥ The Heart of the Matter

The second stage of VSED is similar to active labor in childbirth, with increased discomfort, exhaustion, and anticipatory fear of what's next to happen. The need for comfort and encouragement is very high in this stage.

Q: What are the characteristics of Stage 2 of VSED:

- This is the most difficult stage for everyone – the Individual dying and their support circle.
- Thirst increases, some delusion, some loss of mental capacity, potential agitation.
- The individual remains in bed with weakness and loss of balance, which are a safety factors.
- Symptom management – important and essential.
- This is the point where one must move forward through the VSED process.

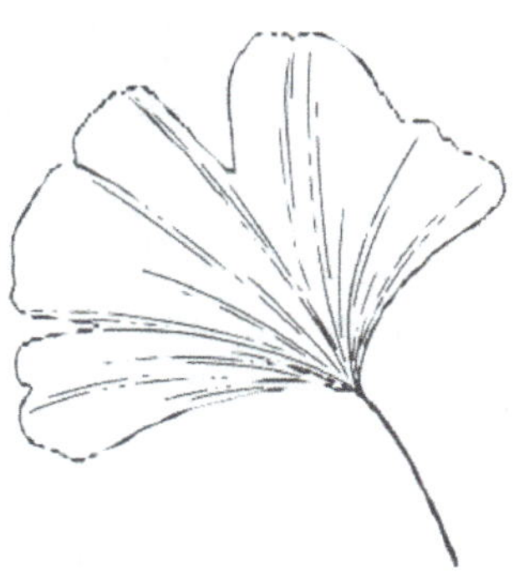

Q: What might the support person might see and hear in Stage 2 of VSED?

- Individual may ask for water – have a plan in place and practice a consistent response.
- Individual may, hopefully, be distracted by music, conversation, visits from favorite animals or people, being read aloud to.
- Individual may sleep for longer periods of time, or be restless, or agitated.
- Individual may sound confused when speaking or may speak with symbolic language, such as "I am going home" or "I need to pack for the trip."
- Individual may be aware of their loss of cognition, such as memory, and express concern about this.
- Because toileting is an ingrained habit, Individual may be resistant to using a bedpan or an incontinent product that allows them to "pee the bed."

Q: What emotions might a support person feel during Stage 2 of VSED?

- Fatigue and concern about the length of this process – "How long will this last?"
- Tendency to self-identify with the Individual in the bed.
- Continued feelings of anticipatory grief as well as gratitude for this time together.
- Concern that their Individual may appear to be "suffering."
- Fear as the Individual becomes more and more confused, with possible delirium.

Q: What can a support person do for their own self-care and soul-care?

- Talk to one's own body and reassure it that it is alive. It is not the body that is dying!
- Talk with death doula about anything seen that is causing distress to oneself or the Individual.
- Refer to this book – knowledge can be comforting.
- Take breaks for yourself.
- Maintain sleep routine habits and continue to eat and drink regularly.
  - Keep in mind who is doing the VSED – eat and drink but away from VSED room or household so no food odors reach the Individual.
- Find amusement in things, it's okay – including death jokes if that feels right.
- Talk with a compassionate listener about what you're experiencing and feeling.
- Be creative – draw, journal, write a poem or song, take pictures.
- Get outside – go for a walk or run, sit in a favorite spot.

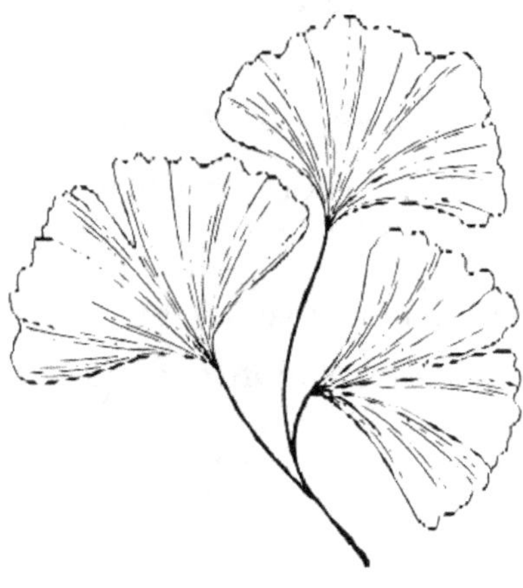

Q: How can the support person be helpful in Stage 2?

- Be a calm, loving presence.
- Help create a visual "focus point" for the Individual, such as a display or altar. Perhaps use a table-top for family pictures, items that are precious to the Individual and reminiscent of their life, flowers and other things of beauty.
- Play music the Individual prefers or read aloud something they have selected and enjoy.
- Assist caregiver with personal care, if appropriate.
- Hold hands with Individual, give foot massage or hand massage, apply moisture to face and lips.
- Eat and drink away from the Individual's room and use a breath mint after eating so there are no lingering smells of food.
- Remember to not bring coffee cups or water bottles into the Individual's room.
- Share words of encouragement and love.
- Greet Individual when arriving and leaving; let them know when you will return.
- Reassure Individual that you are accepting of and not embarrassed by their vulnerability (such as state of undress, use of incontinent products or bedpan, etc.)
- Pass onto caregiver/doula any complaints of nausea, cramping, pain, or discomfort the Individual experiences.

Q: Is VSED still reversible in Stage 2?

* Yes.
* Before an Individual becomes unconscious, the VSED process can be stopped with the ingestion of fluids.
* Note: Medical consultation would be necessary in rehydrating and feeding.

Q: What is the role of the death doula in Stage 2?

* Available on a 24/7 basis to the Individual, support circle and caregivers.
* Is the consistent 'point individual' as a hub for navigating communication and any changes.
* Visits daily to assess the VSED process, encourage the patient, support the family and caregivers.
* Continues to coordinate with hospice staff.
* Reviews caretaker notes each day as well as hospice nurse notes & instructions.
* Encourages family members to eat and sleep regularly for their own self-care.
* Is available to give anticipatory grief care to family and caregivers.
* Explains to family and caregivers what changes they currently notice and what they may see in the succeeding day, giving anticipatory guidance.
* Serves as gate-keeper if necessary for the Individual using VSED.
* Available to deal with the unexpected.

Q: What discomforts can the Individual experience in Stage 2 and what helps?

- Dry mouth and throat: Can be felt because of dehydration – constantly use of vaporizer moisten airway, frequent mouth care, moisturizers to lips and mouth
- Confusion: Can occur as the dehydration process continues – meds, personal care and attention
- Anxiety: Can accompany the confusion – meds, distraction, personal care and attention
- Pain: Medication

Q: What medications are used during Stage 2?

- Liquid Morphine – for difficulty breathing, pain
- Liquid Lorazepam – for anxiety
- Liquid Haloperidol – if needed for delirium
- Fentanyl patch – for pain

Q: What holistic practices are helpful in this stage?

- Acupuncture/acupressure – helpful with nausea and pain
- Massage to feet, hand, face, back – helpful with discomfort, muscle pain, distraction
- Heating pad/frozen packs – helpful with nerve pain, sensation of dryness, intestinal cramping
- Aromatherapy (use a diffuser) – helpful with comfort, distraction
- Healing Touch or Reiki – for general wellbeing and comfort
- Hypnosis – helpful with anxiety, discomfort, even nausea

Stage 3 – End of VSED

Days 7 – 9 + (approximately)

Q: What are the characteristics of Stage 3 of VSED?

- Individual's body is actively dying; organ systems are failing.
- Individual is asleep majority of time, may lapse into coma.
- Ongoing holistic care and comfort measures continue for symptoms.
- The focus of both the death doula and the caregivers moves to those losing a loved one.
- Support circle finalizes plans for death and after-death care.

Q: Is VSED reversible at this stage?

- No. By this time an Individual is so dehydrated they are in a coma and organ failure is happening.

Q: What might the support person see and hear in Stage 3 of VSED?

- Individual's skin may look yellowed and pale, and extremities become mottled as their organ systems begin to shut down.
- Deep sleep to coma for most of the time – may wake suddenly.
- Temperature fluctuations – flush and hot, cold and pale.
- Little or no urine output – urine is dark and can have a strong odor.
- Irregular heartbeat and breathing – may hear gurgling of mucous in back of throat, sometimes referred to as the "Death Rattle."
- Medication will be adjusted as needed.
- Comfort measures continue.

Q: What might a support person feel emotionally at this time?

- Relief that the end is in sight, the journey and struggle is almost over.
- Guilt or concern about being so tired and wanting this experience to be over.
- Worry that the unconscious Individual is unable to verbally express any pain and suffering.
- Struggle with one's own grief, yet feel gratitude that loved one is still present.

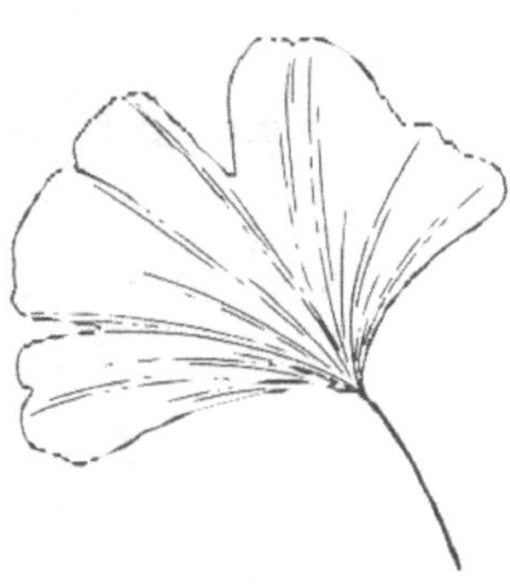

Q: What might a support person do for self-care and soul-care during this?

- Keep communication with one's own body to reassure it that it is quite alive. It is not the body that is dying! This can be done by patting one's arms or legs or giving oneself a hug.
- Talk with death doula about anything seen that is causing distress.
- Refer to this book – knowledge can be comforting.
- Take breaks.
- Maintain sleep routine/habits, continue to eat and drink.
- Get outside – go for a walk or run, sit in a favorite spot.

Q: What can a support person do to be helpful to the Individual in Stage 3?

- Be a quiet, loving presence in the room.
- Assume that the Individual can hear, so continue speaking words of love and encouragement.
- Review with others in the support circle the plans for what happens after death.
- Play music that the Individual prefers or read something that they have selected.
- Assist caregiver with personal care, if all agree.
- Hold hands with your open hand under theirs, or gently rest your hand on the Individual's hand.
- When arriving and leaving the room, gently tell the Individual you are present.
- Alert the caregiver or doula if you sense the Individual is experiencing distress.

Q: What can a support person say to an Individual in a coma?

- **Speak words of love and encouragement**
  - I love you.
  - I'm here with you and here for you.
  - We're all here with you; you are not alone.
  - You are safe.
  - You're dying the way you wished and planned.
  - Your body knows how to do this.
  - It's okay for you to let go.
  - Go with my blessings.
  - I'll always love you.
  - Thank you.

Q: What role does a death doula have in Stage 3 of VSED?

- Available on a 24/7 basis to the Individual, support circle and caregivers.
- Is the consistent 'point individual' as a hub for navigating communication and any changes.
- Visits daily to assess the VSED process, encourage the patient, support the family and caregivers.
- Continues to coordinate with hospice staff.
- Reviews caretaker notes each day as well as hospice nurse notes & instructions.
- Encourages family members to eat and sleep regularly for their own self-care.
- Is available to give anticipatory grief care to family and caregivers.
- Explains to family and caregivers what changes they currently notice and what they may see in the succeeding day, giving anticipatory guidance.
- Serves as gate-keeper if necessary for the Individual using VSED.
- Available to deal with the unexpected.

Q: What physical discomforts can the Individual experience in Stage 3 and what can help?

- Dry mouth and throat: Constant use of vaporizer to moisten airway, frequent mouth care, moisturizers to lips and mouth
- Pain: Medication
- Excessive secretions due to difficulty swallowing: Medication

Q: What medications are more likely used in Stage 3 of VSED?

- Morphine – for pain
- Fentanyl patch – for pain
- Scopolamine (patch) – to dry excess secretions

Q: What holistic practices are helpful in Stage 3 of VSED?

- Healing Touch, Reiki
- Aromatherapy – use a diffuser, or put essential oil on a cotton ball, or use scented candle

Stage 4: Death and After-Death Considerations

♥ The Heart of the Matter

As with a birth, all individual and family relationships are forever changed when death occurs. Transformation takes place.

Q: What are the characteristics of Stage 4 of VSED?

- The task of Stage 4 is to be in the transformation of the present moment.
- There is nothing to do, no hurry, when the last breath comes.
- This is a sacred time, a time of reflection and presence, of gathering the circle
- Other caregivers, if not already in attendance, usually would like to be notified to come.
- Other family members or friends may be summoned, depending on plans made ahead of time.

Q: What might the support person see and hear during Stage 4 of VSED?

- Respectful quiet or silence, also crying or quiet talking.
- Everything stops and pauses – there is no need to rush with anything.
- People may gather around the body or sit quietly in the room.
- Caregivers may clear area of all medical items, which are no longer needed.
- Individual's body relaxes and can still be warm to the touch.
- Pre-arranged plans for bathing and dressing the body may be discussed, possibly altered.
- Over time the body cools and stiffens with rigor mortis, then relaxes again after several hours.
- Circle of family and friends may increase and gather as after-death plans are carried out. These can include a visitation in the home, a ceremony when body leaves the residence, organizing for a home funeral, or arrangements for cremation or burial.

Q: What can the support person do during this time?

- Be a quiet, calming presence.
- Touch the Individual's body, including the face. Hold a hand, stroke the arm.
- Help respond to anyone in room who is grief-stricken and needs to be attended.
- Remind those present of any planned ritual for after-death, including washing/dressing of the body and/or arranging the body and room for a viewing, ceremony or home funeral.
- Help gather necessary items for the planned after-death events.
- Participate in the after-death events as one feels capable.

Q: What is the role of the death doula in Stage 4?

- Be a calming presence.
- Record time of death for hospice and legal documents.
- Make certain hospice is notified with time of death.
- Respond to anyone in room who is grief-stricken and needs support.
- Facilitate the required reporting to authorities if hospice is not involved,
- Help identify who is willing and emotionally capable of assuming pre-determined planned tasks such as bathing and dressing body.
- Guide friends and family through the pre-determined, planned after-death arrangements, including calling funeral home, conducting a leave-taking ceremony as body is removed from the residence, helping coordinate a visitation if done in the home, helping set-up for a home funeral if taking place in the home.
- Remain in touch with family for a pre-determined period of time, to help assess their Individual expression of bereavement and to help process the VSED experience from their perspective.
- Meets with caregivers shortly after the death to gather their perspective of the VSED experience and to help process any challenging aspects of the process.

Q: How is hospice involved after a death?

- There is no hurry to notify hospice services, only to report time of death.
- Hospice often asks if their in-person presence would be helpful at this time.
- Hospice medical director or designate will sign death certificate.
- Hospice will counsel friends and family about the safe disposal of medication.
- Hospice will notify family members about grief-support services provided by hospice.

PRAYER FOR AFTER DEATH
By Olivia Bareham

Blessed One, your life's work is complete and all is forgiven and released.
The purity of love from those gathered here today knows no bounds.
We are here to support you on your way.

Thank you for your gifts of love and service.
Thank you for assisting humanity in the endless evolution toward Love.
We are profoundly grateful.
Go now in peace without hesitation.
You will be loved for always and will never be forgotten.

We call upon all guardian angels, guides and ancestors of this precious soul.
Please lift (her/him/them) on your wings and guide (her/him/them) safely
into the embrace of eternal Love.

Holy Father, Holy Mother, Great Architect of the Universe,
we humbly beseech you to open the gates of heaven
and receive our (name) back into your tender, loving embrace,
until we meet again.

Amen

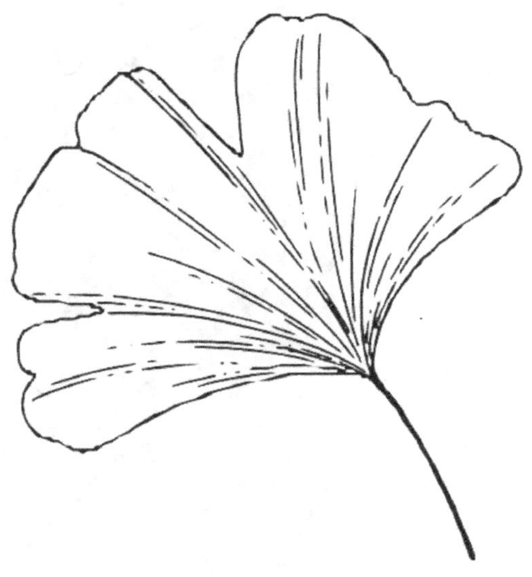

Expanded Resources

Author's Reflections and Notes

Dear Reader,

I wrote this book based on my experience with Individuals who chose to end their suffering by using Voluntarily Stopping and Eating (VSED).

It is meant to inform and encourage those who wish to support someone who has chosen this path of hastening their death.

This book is not a comprehensive clinical overview of VSED, but rather a resource for friends and family as an educational resource, written in non-clinical language.

My hope is that this information will provide knowledge and insight for the supporters, empowering them to care for their loved one with confidence and compassion.

– Nancy Simmers, RN, Death Doula

- **Do you have a question about VSED that is not answered in this book?**

Please email Nancy at nancy.simmers@icloud.com. Your feedback and suggestions are valuable.

- **Do you wish to schedule a presentation or training about VSED?**

If you are a member of a senior residence or are affiliated with a community organization or agency that wants to discuss end-of-life options, feel free to contact Nancy regarding Zoom or in-person presentations about VSED and MAID, Medical Aid in Dying.

- **Are you a death doula?**

Please contact Nancy about pre-ordering her soon-to-be-published, VSED Manual for Death Doulas. She also is available to offer training programs regarding the management of VSED. Contact her at nancy.simmers@icloud.com.

- **Do you know a death doula?**

If you know a death doula, please acknowledge them and spread the word about the valuable services they provide. Feel free to bring this book to their attention.

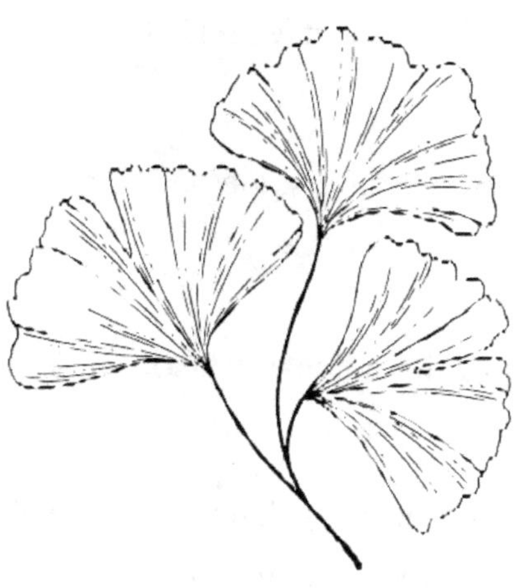

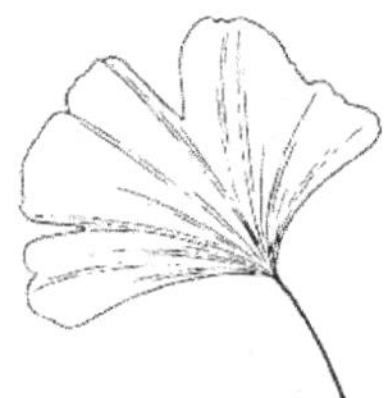

About the Author
Nancy Simmers, BSN, RN, Death Doula

Following a 30-year career as a maternal-child public health nurse and birth doula, Nancy Simmers felt called to serve at the other end of life's continuum. Her work as a death doula began in earnest after attending the first International Death Doula Conference in 2015. Among death doulas from all over the world, she found her purpose and community.

Nancy's focus deepened through her connection with Phyllis Shacter, author of *Choosing to Die*, a memoir chronicling her husband's decision to pursue Voluntarily Stopping Eating and Drinking (VSED) to avoid advanced Alzheimer's. Inspired by Phyllis and the first National VSED Conference in 2016, which she helped to plan, Nancy began specializing in end-of-life options, supporting her first VSED client soon after.

Nancy was also inspired by another mentor and friend, the late Trudy James, a retired chaplain and end-of-life planning champion who was nationally recognized for her work with AIDS patients. After retirement, Trudy founded *Heartworks-Speaking of Dying*, and wrote a comprehensive curriculum covering end-of-life planning and advance directives. With her curriculum, spiritual wisdom and passion for her calling, Trudy trained many facilitators, including Nancy, to offer small, intimate groups that, over a four-week course, became a safe place to talk about death, contemplate end-of-life options, complete advance directives and support one another in discussing with family members their end of life wishes. Nancy now continues this practice with her clients and colleagues.

For nearly a decade, Nancy's doula practice has focused on VSED and Medical Aid in Dying (MAID). She volunteered with End-of-Life Washington, and in 2019, she co-founded VSED Resources Northwest. This nonprofit provides education, advocacy, and consultation on VSED, a legal yet often unsupported end-of-life choice. The organization's website, www.VSEDresources.com, has become a nationally recognized hub for VSED information, expanding from one county in the Pacific Northwest to the rest of the U.S. and beyond.

Recognizing a critical gap in professional VSED guidance, Nancy asked to be included in the team of clinicians who wrote the first-ever American VSED Clinical Guidelines, published in 2023 in *The Journal of Pain and Symptom Management*. She currently co-leads the Last Dance Collective, a local group of death doulas and caregivers specializing in VSED and MAID, with a vision to establish a Death Doula House—a supportive home-like space for Individuals choosing these paths.

Nancy continues to learn from every Individual and family she accompanies, believing that collaboration between death doulas, caregivers, clinicians, and hospices can transform how we approach dying. Her mission is rooted in connection, compassion, and equity—ensuring that everyone, regardless of race, gender identity, poverty, or access to healthcare, has the opportunity to face death with dignity and support.

Through education, advocacy, partnership, and writing, Nancy works to ease fear, honor choice, and break the stigma surrounding end-of-life options like MAID and VSED, helping us all talk more openly about death and plan for it with care and intention.

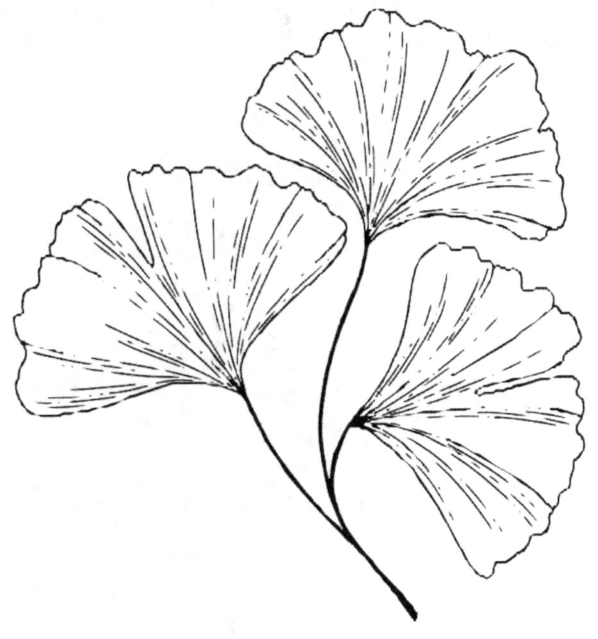

Glossary of Terms

Acupuncture

A form of complementary, wholistic, medicine that involves pricking the skin or tissues with needles. It is used to alleviate pain and to treat various physical, mental, and emotional conditions. Originating in ancient China, acupuncture is now widely practiced in the West.

Advance Directive

Also known as a Healthcare Directive, or Living Will, is a legal document that tells your provider and healthcare agent what treatments you would or would not want if you were permanently unconscious or not expected to recover.

Advocate

To speak for, support, or represent a person or group of people who may need extra help or protection.

Anticipatory Grief

The experience of grief before a loss, often related to an impending death or significant life change. It is a normal response to the realization that a loss is on the horizon and can include a range of emotions and behaviors.

Aquamation

Known also as water cremation, a method of final disposition that uses a mixture of water and an alkali solution, like potassium hydroxide, to break down the body, rather than fire, as used in cremation. This process, called alkaline hydrolysis, gently dissolves the soft tissues, leaving behind the bones, which are then ground into a fine ash, similar to traditional cremation.

Autonomy

Having the freedom and ability to make your own decisions and act independently, without being controlled or influenced by others. It is being able to lead your life according to your own values and desires.

Body Donation

This choice involves pre-registering with a Willed Body Program to allow medical/scientific research on your remains after death. Once accepted, your remains are embalmed and used for research and instruction for about a year. After that, they're cremated and returned to your family. Note that even with pre-registration, your remains may not be accepted for donation due to various reasons. If you choose to donate, have a backup plan in place. Body donation is usually free, and no funeral home or cremation provider is involved.

Capacity

Refers to a patient's ability to understand information related to their medical condition and treatment options, and to make a decision that is consistent with their values and preferences. It is the basis of informed consent and is a functional assessment of a patient's ability to make a specific decision.

Clinical guidelines

Evidence-based recommendations developed by medical experts to assist clinicians in making decisions about patient care. They are intended to improve the quality and effectiveness of care by providing guidance on best practices for specific conditions.

Coma

A deep state of unconsciousness where a person is unresponsive to their environment, including pain, light, and sound. The person may be alive, but they cannot be awakened, and there is little or no brain activity.

Cremation

A process that reduces a body to bone fragments and ash through the application of high heat within a cremation chamber. The remains are then processed and placed in an urn or other container for disposition.

Death doula

Also known as an end-of-life doula or death midwife, is a non-medical professional who provides emotional, physical, and spiritual support to Individuals nearing the end of their lives and their loved ones. They offer companionship, guidance, and practical assistance to help Individuals navigate the dying process and create a more peaceful and meaningful death experience.

Death rattle

A colloquial term for the noisy breathing sound that can be heard as an Individual nears the end of life. It is often described as soft, wet, crackling, moan-like, or gurgling sounds. This sound is caused by the accumulation of fluid in the upper airways, making it difficult for the Individual to clear secretions.

Dehydration

Occurs when one uses or loses more fluid than one takes in, and one's body doesn't have enough water and other fluids to carry out its normal functions.

Delirium

A sudden change in a person's mental state, characterized by confusion, disorientation, and difficulty focusing. It can also involve changes in alertness, hallucinations, and alterations in speech or movement. While it can occur at any age, it's more common in older adults, especially those hospitalized, and can be triggered by various medical conditions, medications, or substance withdrawal. Delirium is often temporary and treatable, especially if the underlying cause is addressed.

Dementia

A condition characterized by progressive or persistent loss of intellectual functioning, especially with impairment of memory and abstract thinking, and often with personality change, resulting from organic disease of the brain.

Diagnosis

The process of identifying a disease, condition, or injury from its signs and symptoms.

Disposition	The "disposition of a deceased body" refers to the final actions taken with a body after death, typically involving burial, cremation, or other methods of disposal. It also encompasses the legal and practical processes of dealing with the remains, including obtaining necessary permits and arranging for the final resting place or scattering of ashes.
DPOA-HC **Durable Power of Attorney for Health Care**	Durable Power of Attorney-Health Care: a legal document that allows you to name someone you trust to make healthcare decisions for you if you become unable to do so yourself. This person, called your health care agent, can consent to, refuse, or withdraw treatment and make other healthcare decisions on your behalf.
DPOA-Finances **Durable Power of Attorney for Finances**	Durable Power of Attorney-Finances: a legal document that allows a person to name a trusted friend or relative to help you with your finances, including buying and selling property, depositing and withdrawing money from accounts, establishing eligibility for public benefits programs and paying bills. Without this, almost all care decisions that involve money or assets will cease until a guardianship is set up, costing thousands of dollars and resulting in a loss of rights and time.
Embalming	The process of introducing a disinfectant solution to the internal environment of the body when someone passes away. It delays changes to the body which occur after death, giving the deceased a more restful appearance and, in some situations, removing some visible effects of the cause of death.

Eulogy

A speech given at a memorial service in memory of a person who has died. The purpose is to recall the defining qualities and highlights of a life lived in a way that benefits the audience, particularly the family.

Fentanyl patch

Fentanyl is a synthetic opioid typically used to treat patients with chronic severe pain or severe pain following surgery. Fentanyl is a Schedule II controlled substance that is similar to morphine but about 100 times more potent. Under the supervision of a licensed medical professional, fentanyl has a legitimate medical use.

Green Burial

Also known as natural burial, is an environmentally sustainable alternative to traditional burial that emphasizes simplicity and a return to nature. It avoids embalming, concrete vaults, and other materials that negatively impact the environment. It typically involves placing the deceased in a biodegradable casket or shroud and interring them directly into the earth, allowing the body to decompose naturally and return to the soil.

Haloperidol

An antipsychotic medicine that works by blocking certain types of nerve (neuron) activity in the brain. This can help with feelings of anxiety.

Hypnosis

A state of focused attention and heightened suggestibility, often used for relaxation, pain management, and behavioral change.

Inanition

A state of malnutrition and can arise from a multiplicity of causes. These include acute infections, impaired cognition, heart failure, dysphagia (swallowing problems), dementia, delirium, depression, malignancies and adverse effects arising from medications.

Incontinent products

Are absorbent materials, pads, or devices used to manage urinary or fecal incontinence, helping Individuals manage leakage and maintain hygiene and comfort. These products come in various forms, including pads, protective underwear, and underpads, designed to absorb and contain bodily fluids.

Informed Choice

Is making a decision based on sufficient knowledge and understanding of the available options, their potential implications, and the relevant factors. It involves having the information needed to weigh risks and benefits, understanding your values and preferences, and making a voluntary decision.

Lorazepam

A drug that is used to treat anxiety and certain seizure disorders, such as epilepsy, and to prevent nausea and vomiting caused by chemotherapy. It belongs to the families of drugs called antiemetics and benzodiazepines.

MAID

Medical Aid in Dying

The practice where a healthcare professional provides a terminally ill patient with lethal medication that the patient can self-administer to end their life. It is a legal practice in 11 jurisdictions in the United States, including Oregon, Washington, Colorado, Vermont, California, and the District of Columbia.

Morphine

Provides significant relief to patients with pain and helps with breathing. Medicating with morphine is beneficial in managing palliative/end-of-life care.

Mottled Skin

Especially near the end of life, is a common sign of poor circulation, often caused by the heart's inability to pump blood effectively. It is a strong indicator that death is imminent.

Prognosis

In medicine, refers to the likely course and outcome of a disease, including the chances of recovery or survival.

Shunting

In medicine, "shunting" refers to the diversion of a fluid, like blood, from its normal path to a different location in the body. Near death, blood supply is shunted to the lungs and heart in a final attempt to sustain life.

Reiki

A complementary therapy that promotes healing by transferring energy from a practitioner to a recipient, aiming to clear energy blockages and restore balance. Practitioners believe that when energy flows freely, an individual experiences improved physical, emotional, and spiritual well-being.

ROI
Release of Information

The primary purpose of a Release of Information (ROI) form is to allow Individuals to authorize healthcare providers to share their protected health information (PHI) with other parties, such as doctors, insurers, or legal representatives. This ensures that information is shared with the right people, for the right reasons, and in accordance with privacy regulations like HIPAA.

Suicide

Death caused by self-directed injurious behavior with intent to die as a result of the behavior.

Symbolic Language

Expressions related to travel or journeys often convey individuals' feelings and understanding of approaching death. This communication allows them to express their emotions, anxieties, and hopes about the afterlife. Travel metaphors, repeated numbers and other connected symbols may be expressed. See *Words at the Threshold* by Lisa Smartt.

Terramation

Also known as human composting or natural organic reduction, is a process that transforms human remains into nutrient-rich soil using natural decomposition. This method involves placing the body in a container with organic materials like straw, alfalfa, and sawdust, where microbial activity breaks down the body over time, resulting in soil.

Unconscious

An unconscious person will be unresponsive to stimuli and appear as if they are asleep, but will not respond to loud noises, being touched, or being shaken.

Voluntary

Proceeding from the will or from one's own choice or consent.

Unremitting

Symptoms or conditions that do not improve over time or that persist continuously.

VSED

Voluntarily Stopping Eating and Drinking

The process of dying by dehydration, fasting from both food and water. It is a deliberate choice to end one's life made by a person with decisional capacity.

Further Reading

VSED Resources Northwest

www.VSEDresources.org

A Non-Profit Organization increasing awareness for legal End of Life Choices, especially VSED

Offering:
- Phone, email & in-person consultations
- Caregiver & Death Doula Referrals
- VSED Presentations & Trainings
- VSED Clinical Guidelines
- VSED Care Plans

End of Life Washington

www.EndofLifeWA.org

A non-profit in WA State that supports and advocates for those facing the end of life; assists with all aspects of end-of-life decision making, including VSED. Guides care seekers to help navigate through the end-of-life.

The VSED Handbook
Kate Christie

In this short, comprehensive guidebook, Kate Christie details the steps her family took when her late mother Jane chose a peaceful death via VSED to escape the final brutal stages of Alzheimer's disease.

In clear, non-clinical language, Christie offers a plan for anyone considering hastening their death. She emphasizes the importance of planning, palliative and hospice care, and medical and doula support. She also describes what to expect from each stage of the VSED process and highlights the challenges and unexpected gifts of accompanying her mother on her final journey.

As she notes, a peaceful death free of suffering is possible with VSED, but only with planning, perseverance, and the support of a trusted team.

Available on Amazon in eBook and paperback.

ISBN-13: 978-0-9853677-9-4
Second Growth Books, Seattle

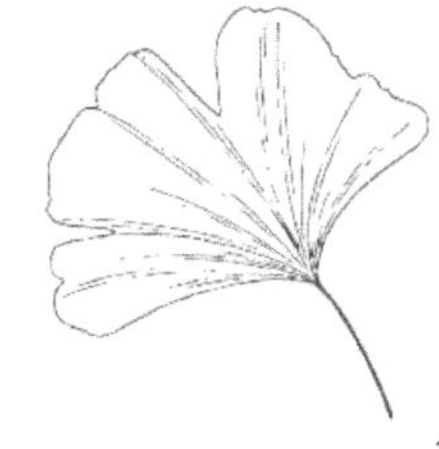

Choosing to Die, A Personal Story
Phyllis Shacter

Phyllis Shacter courageously shares the personal story written about VSED (voluntarily stopping eating and drinking). This memoir and guidebook follows the journey she took with her husband, Alan, once he decided to VSED so he didn't have to live into the late stages of Alzheimer's disease. This is their love story, their partnership, the brave territory they traversed, including how they prepared themselves with proper medical and legal guidance.

They knew they were paving the way for others who would follow in their footsteps. Every detail is shared, including what happened to Alan during the nine-and-a-half days it took for him to die, and how the experience transformed Phyllis. This book is for anyone who wants a deeper understanding of end-of-life choices, and especially for anyone who has been diagnosed with a degenerative disease. www.PhyllisShacter.com

Available on Amazon in paperback.

ISBN 9 781543 173161
Amazon

VSED: A Compassionate, Widely Available Option for Hastening Death
Edited by T. Quill, P. Menzel, T. Pope and J. Schwarz

VSED is a compassionate option that respects patient choice. Despite its strongly misleading image of starvation, death by VSED is typically peaceful and meaningful when accompanied by adequate clinician and/or caregiver support. Moreover, the practice is not limited to avoiding unbearable suffering, but may also be used by those who are determined to avoid living with unacceptable deterioration such as severe dementia. But VSED is "not for everyone."

This volume provides a realistic, appropriately critical, yet supportive assessment of the practice. The volume's integrated, multi-professional, multi-disciplinary character makes it useful for a wide range of readers: patients considering present or future end-of-life options and their families, clinicians of all kinds, ethicists, lawyers, and institutional administrators.

Available on Amazon

ISBN 978-0-19-008073-0
Oxford University Press

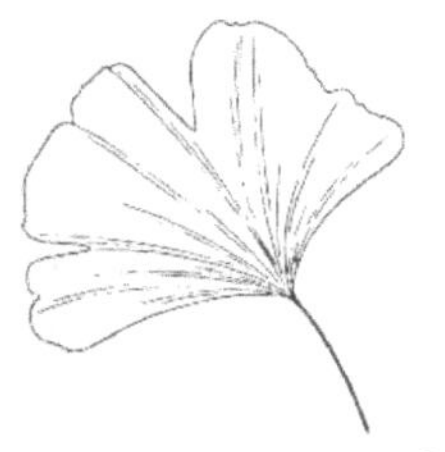

Dignity in Dying: A Thoughtful Approach to Voluntary Stopping Eating and Drinking
Peter M. Abraham, BSN, RN

In Dignity in Dying, Peter M. Abraham, BSN, RN, offers a compassionate and comprehensive guide to VSED as an end-of-life option. This book is essential for anyone considering VSED, whether facing a terminal illness or experiencing unbearable suffering. Abraham provides a clear and empathetic exploration of VSED, emphasizing autonomy, dignity, and comfort.

Through real-life case studies, Abraham illustrates the profound impact of VSED on patients and their families, offering insights into the emotional and ethical considerations involved.

Readers will find practical guidance on preparing for VSED, including the importance of medical consultation, legal considerations, and the role of advance directives. The book also delves into the physical process of VSED, providing a detailed overview of the stages and symptoms to expect. Abraham offers strategies for managing symptoms such as thirst, delirium, and anxiety, ensuring that comfort is maintained throughout the process. The book underscores the importance of palliative and hospice care, which can provide essential support and symptom management.

Ethical considerations are thoughtfully addressed, with discussions on autonomy, self-determination, and the ethical debates surrounding VSED.

Available on Amazon
ISBN-13 979-8335403405

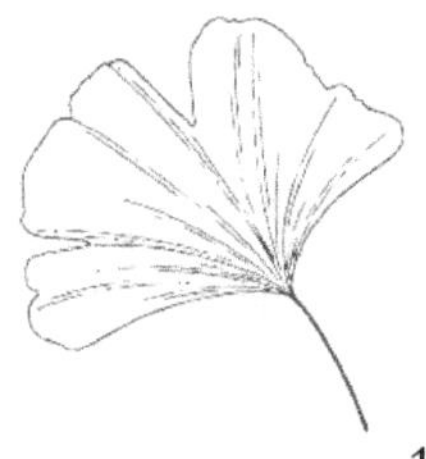

Appendices

VSED Preparation Checklist

☐ **Determine medical support**

- Note and record names and contact numbers for Individual's provider.
- Ask if Individual has spoken with provider about VSED.
  - Determine if provider is supportive.
  - If not, request referral to supportive provider.
- Identify complementary/holistic providers the Individual has previously seen.
- Review advance directive (living will) and current, signed POLST.

☐ **Complete all legal work**

- Release of Information (ROI) Authorization signed, copied, so medical information can be shared.
- Advance Directive (sometimes called a Living Will)
- VSED Advance Directive, specific for VSED. see Appendix V, page 119.
- POLST (MOLST, COLST) completed, signed by provider, and copied.
- Release and Assumption of Risk document for caregivers and doula.
- Identify Individual's legal healthcare agent (Durable Power of Attorney for Heath care).
  - If not supportive of VSED, choose another DPOA-HC.
  - Record and have at the ready the contact numbers for DPOA-HC.
- Legal Will or estate planning completed, if desired and needed.
- Durable Power of Attorney for Finances (DPOA-F)
- Create two videos:
  - Longer video (2-3 minutes) for legal purposes, added to VSED Advance Directive.
  - Shorter video (1 minute), made on cell phone, for reminder to be used during VSED process if Individual requests food or water.

☐ Choose VSED coordinator, trusted friend or death doula, who will:

- Coordinate the whole team – family members, caregivers, hospice, friends, faith community representative – throughout the VSED event.
- Set and maintain an atmosphere of peace and calm.
- Embody compassion and follow the Individual's lead.
- Link with all team members: PCP, hospice, caregivers, holistic practitioners.
- Consistently assess the needs of client, family, caregivers throughout VSED event.
- Serves as the gate keeper to Individual, protecting them from stress and agitation.
- Educate support team about the dying process, VSED process.
- Help Individual prepare an after-death plan prior to start of VSED.

☐ Choose point person for the Individual

- A consistent spokesperson, someone the Individual knows and trusts who will be called to speak with Individual if requests for food or fluids are repeatedly made. This might be family member, friend or the death doula.

☐ Select caregivers

- Discuss importance of full-time caregivers.
- Discuss preference for caregivers:
  - Experienced with end-of-life and VSED.
  - Available consistently for two-week period.
  - Non–family care members, if possible.
- Discuss the financial cost of caregivers.
- Sign Release and Assumption of Risk document, if desired.

☐ Choose the VSED start date or personal markers

- Start date may be determined by such factors as deterioration of physical condition or mental capacity, the availability of medical professionals and caregivers, possible conflict within the family, sudden decline in the quality of life, and other human considerations.
- Markers are behaviors that can be tracked over time and may indicate a decline in quality of life or competency that can suggest it is time for starting VSED.

☐ Complete Comforting Things List

- These are ways of distracting Individual by using senses of sight, touch, smell, hearing.

☐ Confirm Hospice referral

- Determine if referral is best made by healthcare provider or Individual or death doula.
- Ask that hospice intake be conducted before VSED start date, if possible, and with death doula in attendance.
- If possible, obtain hospital bed before VSED start date.

☐ Select physical space

- Identify a safe, comfortable 'nest' in which to receive care.

☐ Consider ways of preparing emotionally and of completing legacy work

☐ Consider and determine desire for spiritual support

- Make plans to honor personal faith traditions, before-during-after VSED.

☐ Consider and determine desire for cultural support

- If appropriate, make specific plans to observe or honor personal cultural traditions.

☐ Finalize selection of supportive circle of friends and family

- Identify, contact, and engage friends and family so they are prepared to support the Individual.

☐ Gather equipment and supplies

☐ Prepare the body physically

- Decrease calorie intake over 4-5 days to facilitate the fast.
- May use an enema to clear the colon before the VSED start date.

☐ Decide about after-death arrangements

- Finalize plan for immediately after death (alone time, washing of body, shrouding, vigiling, ceremony for leaving home).

☐ Plan for what happens to Individual's body

- Options may include traditional burial, green burial, cremation, aquamation, terramation, or body donation.

☐ Plan for funeral, celebration of life, memorial

☐ Final to-do list

- Remove all food and all cooking smells from the house.
- Set up 'nest' area including hospital bed with caregiver supplies, pictures, personal memorabilia, things of beauty and personal significance.
- Review personal role and schedule of support team and caregivers.
- Place in a binder the schedule for caregivers and support team members for easy reference.
- Assemble all VSED related legal paperwork in a binder for easy access.
- Verify that Hospice is on standby and notify hospice of start date.
- Have Individual complete an intestinal cleanse (enema) before start date.

☐ Acknowledge the start date, the beginning of VSED, in a personal way that is meaningful to Individual and their support circle, including caregivers & death doula.

Preferred Comfort Measures & Pleasures to help with VSED

Choosing to stop eating and drinking deprives a person of a major source of nutrition, energy, comfort, stimulation, and pleasure. Focusing on the awareness of other senses can help reduce the loss of that fifth sense and can help distract the person from the discomfort of dry mouth and throat while still providing comfort and pleasure.

Please use the following suggestions to help select ways in which comfort and pleasure can be used to prepare for the days ahead. Review it with a friend or family member. Let those in your support circle know what is comforting and pleasing!

Things to hear
- Conversation – about anything, familiar voices
- Hearing and retelling family stories
- Being read to: favorite books, poems, favorite children's books, letters, cards, and newspaper
- Remembering and discussing events from childhood, births, parenting, jobs, holidays, romance, life challenges, celebrations
- Favorite radio program or announcer
- Podcasts, Pandora
- Listen to music: radio, CDs, singing
- Contact Threshold Singers to come and sing at bedside
- Hire a therapeutic harpist
- Make music – sing, keyboard, instrument
- Favorite types of music through one's lifetime

Things to see, observe, watch

- View from window
- Pictures of cherished people
- Collection basket of natural things: feathers, stones, shells, seeds
- Favorite pictures – of celebrations, milestones, people, pets
- Look at pictures together, in photo album
- Comics
- Cards and letters, saved or new
- TV or other electronics
- Favorite movies
- Projected light images
- Fish in aquarium
- Fire in a fireplace

Things to smell

- Essential oils in a diffuser
- Aftershave cologne
- Loved one's perfume
- Flowers
- Burning scented candles
- Favorite soap
- Favorite body lotion
- Woodburning in a fireplace
- Fresh air, rain

Things to touch

- Hands, faces, bodies of loved ones
- Small basket filled with natural things: feather, stones, shells, seeds
- Pets
- Stuffy
- Doll or toy
- Blanket or shawl
- Cards and/or letters
- Hand massage, foot massage

Things to do together

- Sit quietly and be present
- Cuddle in bed
- Hold hands
- Hug
- Body massage, foot massage, hand massage
- Pedicure, manicure
- Put together puzzles
- Play card games, board games
- Write a legacy letter to grandchildren, best friends
- Draw, paint, watercolor

Bedclothes

- Clean sheets, sun-dried
- Big down coverlet
- Favorite quilt or blanket
- Comfy pillows
- Sheepskin

Places to sit

- Outside chair, swing, hammock
- Rocking chair
- Recliner or couch
- Favorite chair

Create a nest

- Room with a view, natural light
- Windows that can open for fresh air or sound of rain
- Drapes or curtains that can be opened or closed
- Overhead light
- Small lamps with soft light
- Candles
- Nightlight

Things to wear

- Favorite slippers
- Fuzzy socks
- PJs, nightshirt, nightgown
- Shawl, scarf
- Favorite hat
- Gloves, with or without fingers
- Bed jacket

List of Supplies and Equipment for VSED

The following is a list of equipment and supplies very helpful to have during a VSED. Many of these supplies can be procured through hospice.

Safety and accessibility
- Hospital bed (adjustable up and down)
- Bedside commode
- Urinal
- Walker
- Cool air humidifier
- Light-weight wheelchair
- Bath & shower seat
- Baby monitor

Linens
- Mattress topper (preferably with oscillating air)
- Stretchy mattress sheets
- Twin bed sheets
- Bath blankets
- Washcloths
- Towels
- Draw sheets

Personal care supplies
- Incontinent products
- Lip balm
- Lotion
- Eye drops
- Toilet wipes
- Large bath wipes
- Hair-washing supplies
- Gait belt
- Needle-less syringes for meds
- Atomizer spray bottles for misting

Other
- Vigil candles (flameless)
- Linens for vigil
- Massage table for after-death vigil, if desired
- Body wash for after-death vigil, if desired

Script to Use if Someone Choosing VSED Asks for Water

The slightest amount of fluid will increase the time it takes for a body to die of dehydration. This includes sips of water, ice chips, water used to flush an IV port or a rectal catheter used to administer medication, or even a vaporizer positioned close to a person and aimed directly at the face, running 24/7.

It is this person's choice and decision to voluntarily stop eating and drinking. It is their right to change their mind at any point as long as they have mental capacity. If they no longer have mental capacity (evidenced by delirium, hallucinations, severe confusion) the DPOA-HC must be consulted, as they have the authority to speak for the person they represent.

> Discuss and practice this process with VSED person, their caregivers, their family, prior to start of VSED. Document the discussion date and practice date.
>
> Date discussed: _____________Date practiced: ______________Initials: _______

This is the suggested process to use if the Individual should ask for something to drink or eat:

1) Confirm that a drink (or food) is what is being requested:
"Person's name, are you asking for a drink of water?
I want to remind you that you have chosen to stop eating and drinking.
How about we freshen your mouth and get you more comfortable
instead?"

**2) If freshened mouth, repositioning and conversation does not
diminish the request for fluids:**
"Person's name, you're asking again for a drink of water. I want to remind
you that you chose to stop eating and drinking. You may have a drink, but
that will mean your VSED will last longer. Let me freshen your mouth
and help with some medication."

**3) If medication does not help diminish the discomfort / thirst /
dry throat and pharynx, say:**
"Person's name, I know it's tough to have such a dry mouth and nose.
You're asking for water again. You may have something to drink but first
let me play the little video you made to help remind yourself of your
decision to stop eating and drinking. Let's watch together."

[Play the video at full volume and pause to note any response.]

4) If person still wants something to drink, say:
"You may have (ice chips) or a drink of water now but this will slow your
progress with VSED. Do you want to take that risk or shall we try all
these things again? Or do you want to stop this whole VSED Process?"

**Always keep in mind that the person doing VSED has the right to
stop at any point.
It may be necessary for the person to 'experience' VSED once
before committing to it.**

VSED Advance Directive

** Please go to www.washingtonlawhelp.org/VSED to fill out the most updated version of this directive. It is the preferred way to access the directive.

** A copy of the VSED Directive, for reference purposes, follows this page.

The National VSED Advance Directive Committee

This committee developed a better advance directive that instructs either stopping of eating and drinking (VSED) or minimal comfort feeding (MCF) under conditions that the patient/principal specifies. The Committee's VSED advance directive is available from the Northwest Justice Project, www.washingtonlawhelp.org/VSED

Members of the Committee

The National VSED Advance Directive Committee includes five members from different disciplines, professions, and locations.

- Philosopher, Paul Menzel
- Former EOLWA executive director, Robb Miller
- Estate Planning attorney, Erin Mae Glass
- Law professor, Lisa Brodoff
- Bioethicist, Thaddeus Pope

The VSED Directive

A copy of the Advance Directive for VSED is printed on the following pages. However, the Committee recommends accessing the directive through the website for Northwest Justice Project because it has guided menus that will complete the form for you based on your responses.

Several end-of-life advocacy organizations have been recommending the Committee's Advance Directive for VSED. Indeed, even organizations that developed and distributed their own directives now use this one.

- End of Life Washington
- Final Exit Network
- VSED Resources Northwest
- Full Circle of Living & Dying
- Tender Doula

VSED Advance Directive

Advance Directive for
Voluntary Stopping of Eating and Drinking
(VSED Directive)

My name is _________________________________ My date of birth is ___________.

As an adult with decision-making capacity, I have the right to direct my treatment and care, even if those choices lead to an earlier death. This includes the right to refuse medical treatment and the right to refuse oral food and drink. I have thought carefully about the circumstances in which I would want to stop prolonging my life with eating and drinking.

This directive instructs my health care agent or other legal decision-maker ("decision-maker") and all caregivers how to act on my behalf to ensure that my wishes for stopping eating and drinking are carried out.

1. Voluntary stopping of eating and drinking (VSED)

When I meet the conditions I have selected in section 2 (below) and can no longer feed myself:

- Do not help me with eating and drinking (by spoon-feeding, for example).
- Do not verbally or physically encourage or persuade me to eat or drink.
- Do not put food or liquids in my mouth.

2. Conditions for starting VSED

I want to start VSED when I have a serious and irreversible illness or chronic condition that will not significantly improve (even if it is not terminal), and when I meet (*initial one*) **at least one** of the conditions I select below.

___**all** of the conditions I select below (*initial all that apply*):

___I cannot communicate with others beyond a few words, eye movements, etc.

___I do not recognize close family and friends.

___I am indifferent to being fed, no longer want to eat or drink, and show no signs of enjoying eating and drinking.

___I do not open my mouth to receive food and drink, or I turn my head away when offered food or drink.

___I usually refuse food or drink

___I frequently inhale or choke on food or drink.

___The following additional conditions or situations:

____

____

____

____

3. If my decision-maker thinks my quality of life is still good when it is time to start VSED

If my decision-maker thinks my quality of life is still good enough and I seem comfortable or happy, my decision-maker (*initial one*):

___**must follow this directive and start VSED.** I have given a lot of thought to this decision and insist that my wishes be followed.

___may choose **not** to follow this directive. **I understand this means some or all of my choices may not be honored.**

4. Palliative care – relief from pain and discomfort

If food and drink are being withheld, I want palliative care to manage any pain or discomfort from my illness and from not eating and drinking (relief from dehydration, for instance).

I want palliative sedation if necessary to manage pain and discomfort (*initial one*):

__**even if** it makes me unconscious.
__**but not** to the point of unconsciousness.

5. If I express the desire to eat or drink

If eating and drinking has stopped, but I repeatedly show by words or gestures that I want to eat or drink, I want my caregivers to reassess my palliative care and (*initial one*): __continue to withhold all help with eating and drinking.

__give me only enough food and drink to avoid discomfort, even if it's not nutritionally adequate (also known as 'minimal comfort feeding'). **I understand this approach will likely prolong my dying process.**

6. Medical facilities and providers that will not honor this directive

Before I receive care from a medical facility or provider (including my physician or residential hospice, or long-term care facility), I want the facility or provider to confirm it will follow the instructions in this directive. If the medical facility or provider will not follow the instructions in this directive due to moral, ethical, or other reasons, my decision-maker should make all reasonable efforts to make sure I get care from a facility or provider that will.

(Initial if selected)

___**After** I am admitted or receiving care, if a facility or provider will not honor the instructions in this directive, my decision-maker should make all reasonable efforts to make sure I get care from another facility or provider that will. I understand this means I may be transferred to another medical facility or living situation that might cost more or be less convenient.

If a medical facility or provider will **not** follow this directive due to legal or institutional barriers, I want to be given only enough food and drink to avoid discomfort even if not nutritionally adequate (also known as 'minimal comfort feeding').

7. Dispute resolution

My decision-maker will resolve any disagreement about the instructions in this directive and/or whether the conditions I have chosen have been met.

If no decision-maker is available, then I want my medical providers to make these decisions if that is legally allowed.

If any part of this directive is determined to be legally invalid, all other parts should be honored.

8. Health care decision-maker

___I have named a health care decision-maker in the following legal document *(initial one and attach a copy, if possible)*:

___Power of Attorney for Health Care
___Other document *(name)*:
___I have **not** yet named a health care decision-maker.

I intend this directive to supplement any existing documents about my end-of-life care. This directive does not revoke any existing documents except with respect to receiving food and liquid by mouth, in which case this directive shall govern.

I have the following other documents about advance planning or end-of-life wishes:

Name: ____

Name: ____

Name: ____

Name: ____

9. Liability Waiver

I voluntarily assume any and all risk associated with my choice to use VSED as an end-of-life option. I release all persons, including my health care decision-makers, medical providers, caregivers (including but not limited to my physicians, nurses, care facilities, doulas, or personal care providers, etc.), and family members and other loved ones from any and all liability that could result from any and all actions they may take in good faith reliance on my wishes as described in this directive. This includes my express release of civil liability and my strongly held wish that they **not** be subject to any criminal or disciplinary sanctions.

Further, I direct my estate to hold harmless and indemnify my health care decision-makers, medical providers, caregivers, family members, and other loved ones for acts done according to this advance directive in good faith.

Finally, I wish to make it clear that I am making this directive of my own free will and am doing so intentionally to ensure that my medical care is consistent with my stated wishes. As a result, I regard any action taken to undermine my wishes as described in this directive as medical battery and authorize my surrogate and/or my estate to pursue such a claim on my behalf.

11. Capacity

I am making this VSED Directive because if I cannot make decisions for myself, I want my decision-makers, medical and long-term care providers, caregivers, family, and other loved ones to honor every part of this directive.

I am of sound mind. I am voluntarily signing this VSED Directive and understand what it means. I make this advance directive of my own free will, and I have the mental and emotional capacity to do so.

I understand that honoring this directive might cause me to die sooner than if I received help with eating and drinking.

[Sign only in the presence of a notary or qualified witnesses]

____

Date   Signature

____

Print name

➢ **Notarization and Witnessing**

While it is best to have this document both notarized and witnessed, in most places this document is legally binding with either one or the other.

Notarization

State of ______________________________

County of ____________________________

Signed or attested before me on (*date*): ______________________

by (*name*): ____

____
Signature of Notary
Notary Public for the State of
Washington.
My commission expires ____________.

Statement of Witnesses

I, the witness, declare that the person who signed or acknowledged this VSED Directive:

- Is personally known to me
- Signed or acknowledged this VSED Directive in my presence
- Appears to be of sound mind and under no duress, fraud, or undue influence

I also declare that I am over 18 years of age (19 in Alabama) and that I am:

- **Not** the person's health care agent, decision-maker, or alternate decision-maker
- **Not** the person's health care provider, including an owner or operator of their long-term care, residential, or community care facility
- **Not** an employee of the person's health care provider
- **Not** financially responsible for the person's health care
- **Not** an employee of a life or health insurance provider for the person
- **Not** related to the person by blood, marriage, or adoption
- **Not** a beneficiary of any legal instrument, account, or benefit plan of the person
- **Not** a creditor of the person or entitled to any part of their estate under a will or codicil, by operation of law

(Some states may have different rules about who may be a witness. Unless you know your state's rules, please follow the above.)

Witness 1

____
Signature

____
Print Name

____
Address

____
Phone

Witness 2

____
Signature

____
Print Name

____
Address

____
Phone

VSED Clinical Guidelines

**** Please go to https://www.jpsmjournal.com/article/S0885-3924(23)00565-1/ fulltext to access the Clinical Guidelines for Voluntarily Stopping Eating and Drinking.**

Members of the Writing Group made it possible for the journal article to be available to anyone through 'open access', and thus free-of-charge.

**** A copy of the VSED Guidelines, for reference purposes, follows this page. The VSED Clinical Guidelines for Voluntarily Stopping Eating and Drinking**

These are the first published comprehensive clinical guidelines for voluntarily stopping eating and drinking (VSED) in the United States.

Members of the Clinical Guidelines Writing Group

The Clinical Guidelines for VSED Writing Group includes six members:

1. **Hope Wechkin, MD**, Evergreen Health, Dept of Hospice and Palliative Medicine, Kirkland WA
2. **Robert Maculey, MD**, Oregon Health & Science University, Department of Pediatric Palliative Care, Portland OR
3. **Paul T. Menzel, PhD**, Pacific Lutheran University, Department of Philosophy, Tacoma WA
4. **Peter L. Reagan, MD**, Family Practice, retired
5. **Nancy Simmers, RN, Death Doula,** VSED Resources Northwest, Bellingham WA
6. **Timothy E. Quill, MD**, University of Rochester School of Medicine, Department of Medicine, Palliative Care, Rochester NY

Special Article – **Journal of Pain and Symptom Management**, Vol.66 No.5 November 2023

Clinical Guidelines for Voluntarily Stopping Eating and Drinking (VSED)

Hope Wechkin, MD, Robert Macauley, MD, Paul T. Menzel, PhD, Peter L. Reagan, MD, Nancy Simmers, BS, BSN, RN, and Timothy E. Quill, MD Evergreen Health (H.W.), Department of Hospice and Palliative Medicine, Kirkland, WA; Oregon Health & Science University (R.M.), Department of Pediatric Palliative Care, Portland, OR; Pacific Lutheran University (P.T.M.), Department of Philosophy, Tacoma, WA; Family Practice (P.L.R.), retired; VSED Resources Northwest (N.S.), Bellingham, WA; University of Rochester School of Medicine (T.E.Q.), Department of Medicine, Palliative Care, Rochester, NY

Abstract

As the care of patients with serious illness increasingly emphasizes clarifying goals of care, exploring quality of life, and minimizing patients' symptom burden, voluntarily stopping eating and drinking (VSED) has emerged as a topic of increasing interest for patients who face a diminishing quality of life. It is an option for those with serious illness that is legal in every state in the country, but for which there are few published comprehensive guidelines—and none specific to the American medical system—even as public awareness and the number of inquiries regarding this action increase. In addition to the ethical questions raised by the practice and support of VSED, there are also clinical, logistical, institutional, social, religious, spiritual, and administrative considerations for clinicians who are asked to respond to patients' inquiries about VSED and who discuss this option in end-of-life care. With these clinical guidelines, we seek to provide practical recommendations for clinicians who consider providing support to their patients who contemplate and/or undertake this effort to hasten death. J Pain Symptom Manage 2023;66:e625 −e631. © 2023 The Authors. Published by Elsevier Inc. on behalf of American Academy of Hospice and Palliative Medicine. This is an open access article under the CC BY-NC-ND license (http://creativecommons.org/licenses/by-nc-nd/4.0/)

Key Words

Voluntarily stopping eating and drinking (VSED), clinical guidelines, quality of life, patient autonomy, hastened death, end of life (EOL)

Key Message

These are the first published comprehensive clinical guidelines for voluntarily stopping eating and drinking (VSED) in the United States.

Introduction

With palliative care's growth around the world over the last several decades, the care of many individuals with serious illness has increasingly focused on clarifying their goals of care and attending to their pain and nonpain symptoms. As discussions about quality of life have become more common, so too have patients' questions regarding their options for avoiding an existence characterized by what they determine to be an unacceptable quality of life. A growing number of patients, family members, and clinicians have inquired about the option of voluntarily stopping eating and drinking (VSED), and while there are no laws preventing a person from taking this action, there are also no published comprehensive guidelines in the United States or Great Britain to assist clinicians when responding to inquiries about this option.1 As a group of clinicians and academicians from across the United States, we have fielded many inquiries about VSED and have come to recognize the need for pragmatic guidance for clinicians on this topic. In response to this need, we developed a set of clinical guidelines that provides practical assistance for clinicians practicing in multiple settings and specialties. Considerable debt is owed to the Royal Dutch Medical Association (KNMG) and the Dutch Nurses' Association (V&VN) which have published a comprehensive guide for physicians, nurses, and other caregivers to help them in assisting patients who aim to hasten death by stopping eating and drinking.2 The following clinical guidelines were developed in part to adapt this work to the American context, in which laws (such as those pertaining to medical aid in dying, not to mention euthanasia), institutional structures (such as the hospice system of care and long-term care facilities), and attitudes differ from those in the Netherlands.

Because our aim was to develop practical guidelines that could be used efficiently by busy clinicians, our work group included both academicians (P. T. M., R. M., and T. E. Q.)—the latter two of whom also worked extensively in both palliative medicine and clinical ethics—as well as nonacademic clinicians. These clinicians have worked for many years with patients seeking assistance with VSED and include a family physician (P. R.), a palliative medicine physician and hospice medical director (H. W.), and a nurse doula who has attended the deaths of many patients who completed VSED and who frequently receives inquiries from patients and clinicians regarding this practice (N. S.). T. E. Q. and P. T. M. are also two of the coeditors of a recent textbook analyzing VSED from clinical, ethical, legal, and institutional perspectives.3

After performing a comprehensive literature review, our group met 18 times between February 2022 and May 2023 to prioritize and develop these guidelines. On two separate occasions, we submitted our guidelines for review to colleagues with expertise in law (Pope), clinical medicine (Gruenewald, Horowitz, Sandler), public policy (Miller), and biomedical ethics (Diekema, Tate).

Definition of VSED

VSED is a deliberate, self-initiated action by a patient with decision-making capacity (DMC) to hasten death in the setting of suffering refractory to optimal palliative interventions, prolonged dying that the person finds intolerable, or expected deterioration or suffering due to an irreversible illness, that the person regards as unacceptable.4 This action is typically undertaken by a patient with a serious illness associated with a life expectancy of months or years. VSED is characterized by the exercise of a specific choice at a specific time and is dependent on the patient having sufficient decisional capacity at the time that VSED is initiated.

VSED is clinically distinct from comfort feeding only, an approach to the care of patients with advanced illness that does not require decisional capacity. It is also distinct from voluntarily stopping eating and drinking by advance directive (VSED-AD), which is undertaken when patients no longer have decisional capacity but is consistent with preferences and instructions indicated in the past. The additional complexities of VSED-AD incurred by lack of real-time DMC as well as full comprehension of what is occurring are beyond the scope of these guidelines.

When VSED is Considered

Ethical Considerations VSED is legal in the United States and may be undertaken by patients with a clearly-defined terminal illness associated with a prognosis of months to several years. 1,4,5 It may also be sought by a patient who has a diagnosis, such as dementia, that is associated with progressive decline and a prognosis of many years as well as an anticipated quality of life deemed by the patient to be unacceptable.

The ethical questions raised by supporting a patient with a longer prognosis are not the focus of these clinical guidelines; however, clinicians should be aware that ethical concerns associated with providing clinical support for VSED generally increase with patients whose natural life expectancy is greater.6 Comprehensive evaluation of the patient's reason for seeking VSED is especially important in these situations, as this may identify aspects of suffering, including mental health and spiritual issues that can be addressed and ameliorated. Patients may benefit from appropriate therapy and support and should be encouraged to explore these options before pursuing VSED.

DMC is required for a patient to begin VSED. Ethical concerns increase when DMC is unclear, such as in the case of mental health disorders, especially if not optimally treated. Clinicians must verify that the patient truly understands the diagnosis, as well as the risks, benefits, and alternatives to VSED. When evaluating a request to provide clinical support for VSED, a clinician should seek to understand the patient's reasons for considering VSED.

The clinician should confirm that the patient is not being coerced, and that VSED is aligned with the patient's own values.

In order to demonstrate capacity to pursue VSED, a patient should be able to indicate the following:

- An understanding of the underlying diagnosis and prognosis without VSED.
- An understanding of the potential physical challenges associated with VSED, including thirst and dryness of the mouth and throat, as well as the extent to which those can be managed.
- Consistency over time in choosing to pursue VSED.
- An understanding of the social and emotional challenges that may accompany VSED.

Finally, clinicians may struggle with their own roles and responsibilities when responding to patients' inquiries about VSED. They may also be uncertain as to whether they should introduce VSED to patients as one of many "potentially relevant treatment options." [5] While it is beyond the scope of these guidelines to address all of the arguments favoring and opposing clinician support of patients pursuing VSED, consultation from specialists in psychiatry, palliative medicine, and/ or clinical ethics should be strongly considered when there is ambiguity pertaining to the patient's mental health, DMC, and/or the clinician's role in VSED.

Current Symptom Management

VSED is usually pursued in response to suffering associated with symptoms resistant to optimal palliative interventions or a quality of life that is unacceptable to the patient and cannot be improved by palliative care. Therefore, prior to and during evaluation of VSED as a potential choice, all reasonable palliative options should be offered, including those addressing mental, emotional, and spiritual well-being. It is ultimately the patient's choice whether that care is sufficiently effective to lead them not to choose VSED.

VSED is usually pursued in response to suffering associated with symptoms resistant to optimal palliative interventions or a quality of life that is unacceptable to the patient and cannot be improved by palliative care. Therefore, prior to and during evaluation of VSED as a potential choice, all reasonable palliative options should be offered, including those addressing mental, emotional, and spiritual well-being. It is ultimately the patient's choice whether that care is sufficiently effective to lead them not to choose VSED.

Prognosis With and Without VSED

Because VSED can be accompanied by physical, emotional, social, and logistical challenges, patients should be provided with the most accurate prognostic information available without VSED being undertaken.

Since it takes time to complete VSED, pursuit of this option is rarely useful for patients with days to a very few weeks remaining to live and severe physical symptoms refractory to conventional symptom management methods. In such cases, specialty palliative care and/or hospice consultation with intensive symptom management is advised. Clinicians and patients should be aware that the general range of survival once VSED has begun is 7 −21 days, most commonly 10−14, recognizing that estimates should be tailored to the individual patient's clinical status.[2,3,5,7]

Anticipating Difficulties Once VSED Has Begun

It is important for those contemplating VSED to understand that once begun, VSED may pose physical, emotional, and ethical challenges for patients, family members, and caregivers. Patients' resolve to continue VSED may fluctuate once they have begun the process.[8,9] Additionally, a patient's ability to fully understand and articulate their choices regarding their care may begin to decline after VSED has started, particularly in the late stages. Therefore, patients are encouraged to thoroughly discuss and document their intention to abstain from nutrition and hydration once VSED has begun, including after DMC has been lost. This is discussed further in section "Addressing ambivalence" below.

Family, Social, Religious, Spiritual, and Caregiving Considerations

Whenever possible, it is important for a patient to have the support of close family members and/or friends. There is anecdotal evidence that lack of family/social support for a patient's decision to pursue VSED may result in increased emotional distress for the patient once the process of VSED has begun. Patients should also be prepared to have caregivers who can provide 24/7 support for up to several weeks. It is generally very difficult for a single caregiver to fulfill this responsibility, and assistance from others, including experienced death doulas and hospice staff, may be extremely beneficial. Because all members of the clinical team may experience additional emotional and moral burdens when caring for a patient whose death is planned, particular attention should be given to their support as well. In addition, some patients may find it important to discuss VSED with their trusted religious and spiritual leaders.

Hospice Support

Hospice programs provide important medical, nursing, social, spiritual, and bereavement support to patients and their families at the end of life, and often play a critical role in providing end-of-life care in the residential setting. Because a prognosis of six months or less is necessary for most patients to access hospice care, most hospices will not provide direct care to patients with a prognosis greater than six months prior to the initiation of VSED. However, many hospices will enroll patients who have already begun VSED. Clinicians are strongly encouraged to contact their local hospice agency to discuss the potential for hospice referral and enrollment of patients who are planning to start VSED.

Where VSED Takes Place

Patients contemplating VSED live in a variety of settings, including institutions such as skilled nursing facilities and adult family homes. Professional staff in institutional settings may have a range of knowledge of and philosophical support for VSED and may feel bound by professional licensure requirements to offer food and hydration on a regular basis. There may remain some uncertainty regarding whether food and hydration constitute medical treatments and therefore may be declined as a whole, or whether they represent "basic" or "ordinary" care, and thus should be offered regularly.3,5 While there is comprehensive guidance that provides a checklist and best practices for longterm care (LTC) facilities to honor residents' requests for VSED support,10 challenges may remain for LTC facility residents who desire support in pursuing VSED. Clinicians are encouraged to advise patients and family members to seek open discussion with facility administrative leadership about ensuring staff support for a patient prior to beginning VSED. If it is not an option for a patient to remain in a LTC facility while pursuing VSED, clinicians should encourage patients and family members to investigate and consider options for private residential living. Similarly, patients who are considering entering a facility and who wish to preserve their future option to pursue VSED may wish to discuss this with facility administrators prior to entry.

When to Begin VSED
See section "Start date" below.

Portable Medical Orders (POLST, MOLST, COLST, etc.)

Portable medical orders for life-sustaining treatment should be completed prior to the start of VSED. These should indicate a patient's preference for code status of "Do Not Resuscitate" (DNR), comfort measures, and, when applicable, no artificial nutrition and hydration.

Durable Power of Attorney for Healthcare

Patients should be encouraged to appoint a durable power of attorney for healthcare (DPA-HC), also referred to as a Health Care Proxy, and to indicate individuals, in order, to serve as back-ups should the primary DPA-HC be unavailable. Parents of adult children should be encouraged to specify which (if any) children, in which order, should serve as DPA-HC. In choosing a DPA-HC, patients should confirm that the person they select is willing to support their intention to pursue VSED.

Patient Advocacy Organizations and Death Doulas

Clinicians are encouraged to familiarize themselves with area patient advocacy organizations that provide resources and support for patients pursuing VSED and to refer patients to these organizations. Additionally, clinicians are encouraged to refer patients to a death doula experienced with VSED, when available, who may provide invaluable coordination and comprehensive support in addition to that provided by family/ friend caregivers and hospice staff

When VSED Has Been Chosen

Preliminary Steps for the Medical Provider

- Review the expected length of the VSED process, including how it may be affected by diagnosis, physical condition, and strictness of adherence, especially avoiding all fluids.
- Advise patients who consume large amounts of alcohol of the risk for alcohol withdrawal syndrome.
- Discuss treatment of pain, anxiety, and other symptoms. Review the possibility that the patient may experience delirium, which—if accompanied by requests for hydration or nutrition—may result in prolonging, delaying, or curtailing the VSED process, as it is difficult and may be inappropriate for caregivers to refuse to provide nutrition or hydration if requested. (see further discussion in section , "Addressing ambivalence.")

- Discuss discontinuation of medical devices, particularly an implanted defibrillator.

Start Date

Deciding when to begin the VSED process is often difficult because of the many details needed to be considered and planned.

Three primary considerations include:

- The acuteness of the underlying disease.
- The time needed to prepare for VSED.
- The possibility of a narrowing window of time during which the patient has sufficient cognitive capacity to initiate VSED.[2,11] It is helpful to guide patients in identifying specific, measurable "markers" of capacity, physical ability, and degree of suffering that would assist the patient in deciding when to start VSED.

Preparations for VSED often include:

- Medical consultation and support.
- Hospice referral and clarification of the hospice's willingness to enroll a patient who intends to pursue VSED.
- Consultation with a death doula experienced with VSED who will support the patient and family throughout the entire process.
- Hiring caregivers, ideally those experienced with VSED
- Legal consultation if there are concerns about family members' or others' support of patient's decision.
- Determining where patient will reside while pursuing VSED.
- Obtaining necessary supplies and equipment, including mist humidifier, mouth lubricant, eye drops, small spray bottle, and mouth swabs.
- Informing chosen family members, friends, and others who comprise a person's inner circle of support of patient's decision, start date, and specific ways in which they can be supportive.

Hospice Enrollment

See section "Hospice support" above. Hospice enrollment can be extremely helpful for patients pursuing VSED. Clinicians are strongly encouraged to contact their local hospice directly to discuss medical eligibility and enrollment.

Environment

See section "Where VSED takes place" above. Careful consideration should be given to a patient's environment. Many people wish to pursue VSED in their own home, surrounded by familiar sights and sounds, personal items, and people they love. This may not be feasible if sufficient caregiving is not available. On the other hand, healthcare facilities, assisted living facilities, and adult family homes may have prohibitions against VSED or may be unable to provide 24/7 caregiving.

Typical Phases

VSED typically involves three stages:

- Early: In the early stages of VSED, the patient is alert and oriented, able to interact with their circle of support, and can easily tolerate or be distracted from occasional hunger pangs and increasing thirst and dryness. Prior to the start of VSED, it is helpful for patients to identify the ways they prefer to be comforted and distracted. Throughout the VSED process, but especially during the early and middle stages, these favored approaches are truly helpful. This is also a time for final important conversations, recollections, sharing of family stories, and celebrating the patient's life.
- 2. Middle: This stage is often the most difficult. With increasing dehydration, the patient becomes weak, fatigued, lightheaded, and begins to sleep for longer periods of time. The patient may suffer from agitation, confusion, and hallucinations. Delirium is not

- uncommon. Medications, massage, and acupuncture may mitigate these symptoms; seizures should always be treated promptly with appropriate medication.
- 3. Transition/late: This stage is marked by loss of consciousness as organ systems fail and is similar to the late dying process in other settings.

Symptom Management

1. Dry mouth and throat. This is by far the most common and troublesome symptom.

Both humidifying the surrounding air and providing meticulous mouth care are important in reducing discomfort. When a patient is conscious, teeth, gums, and tongue should be brushed regularly. In addition, the mouth may be moistened with spritzes of water from an aerosol bottle top or with moistened mouth sponges or artificial saliva, and lips should be lubricated at regular intervals. For patients with decreasing consciousness, moistened mouth sponges, frozen teething rings to hold in the mouth, frozen wet washcloths held to the face, frozen drops of coconut oil, and lip balm can all be helpful. It is important that patients and caregivers are aware that even small amounts of water or ice chips can markedly prolong the dying process, so hydration in any form should be minimized for patients who remain committed to completing VSED. It may help to review the benefits of dehydration, including decreased respiratory secretions, less bother with urination, and decreased edema.

2. Hunger.
Hunger tends to be most intense in the first few days and may correlate with the time of day. Some clinicians report that decreasing intake of calories at least one week prior to beginning VSED can reduce hunger.

We are all used to punctuating our days with meals, so when not eating, days seem much longer.

It is therefore very helpful to provide as much sensory and mental stimulation as the patient desires during this early phase, including visits with loved ones, music, movies, reminiscing over photo collections, etc. Focusing on the other senses can ameliorate the loss of the sensations of taste and oral stimulation. Prior to the start date, patients can be asked to identify ways they derive comfort and pleasure using their other senses by offering a checklist of possible distractions that involve senses other than taste.

3. *Constipation and cramping.* At the beginning of the process, many patients find it useful to do some sort of bowel cleanse to decrease the chance that stool will collect and harden in the colon as dehydration proceeds. Ideally the method chosen would not include a large amount of hydration. Instead, bisacodyl, polyethylene glycol, or enemas can be used.

4. *Medication side effects,* and the effects of withdrawing medications. As dehydration proceeds, blood levels of medications will be affected. There is no substitute for frequent reassessment of symptoms to determine whether medication doses need to be modified. Medications taken solely to reduce long-term health risks should be tapered or discontinued prior to beginning VSED. Additionally, taking oral medications with water may prolong the VSED process. Palliative care, hospice, and/ or pharmacy consultation is recommended to reduce medication burden to the minimum required for comfort, and to develop alternative, nonoral routes of administration (transcutaneous, rectal) of medications essential for comfort when appropriate. Highly concentrated oral/sublingual medications, including opioids for pain or dyspnea, benzodiazepines for anxiety, and antipsychotics for disturbing delusions or hallucinations are recommended.

5. *Muscle soreness and pain.* Early in the process of VSED, patients should be encouraged to remain active if practical and safe. When it is not, providing help with repositioning is useful. A discussion concerning what measures the patient has previously used for comfort (massage, acupuncture, turning, positioning, etc.) can be instructive. One may consider analgesics, benzodiazepines, or other medications as needed, taking care to minimize concomitant liquid intake.

6. *Fatigue and weakness,* lightheadedness, and loss of balance. These are to be expected and will increase as days go by. Safety measures, including the use of a walker and gait belt are advised. As symptoms advance, patient care must be given at the bedside, including toileting with a bedside commode, use of incontinence products, and body care while in bed. These increased needs for assistance should be discussed and planned for with family, loved ones, and/or hired caregivers.

7. *Confusion, anxiety, and agitation.* As dehydration progresses, these symptoms can be extremely distressing to patient and caregivers. Prevention and preparation are key and anticipatory teaching for the patient and caregivers regarding confusion and agitation should be provided

Patients feel secure when their inner circle of support is harmonious and steady. Ideally all family members, at least those who are present, support the patient's decision. The patient's immediate surroundings will also have a calming effect if it contains familiar objects such as a few well-known photos or pictures. Finally, it is reasonable to use anxiolytics and/or antipsychotics for management of confusion, anxiety, or agitation that is refractory to nonpharmacologic interventions.

8. *Hallucinations.* Patients and their caregivers should be apprised of the possibility that hallucinations − or what some call end-of-life dreams and visions − may occur. These may be peaceful, engaging, and comforting for the patient, in which case they should be seen as part of the process of dying rather than as signaling a need for intervention. However, if they cause the patient agitation and distress that does not respond to gentle, loving support, they may be eased with antipsychotic medications.

9. *Final phase.* The final phase of VSED typically lasts one−two days. In this phase, particular attention should be given to nonverbal expressions of pain, restlessness, and agitation. Placement of a Foley catheter may reduce the need for frequent changes of clothing and bedding. Positional changes are often distressing, and so should be minimized. Continued education of family members about the physical changes they see in their loved one is important. It is also helpful to inform caregivers and others present in the room that patients are often able to hear even after they become unresponsive.

Addressing Ambivalence

It is important for caregivers to discuss with the patient the possibility that the patient may at some point request food and drink, and to plan how such a request should be addressed. This plan might include the identification of a specific, trusted person to respond to all such requests and/or a short, rehearsed sentence that reminds the patient of the reason they chose VSED.[4,13] Some patients have found it helpful to make a short video addressing the reasons they chose VSED, which can be used to remind themselves during the process itself. It may even be helpful to practice this plan with the patient and family members before the start date of VSED. Ideally this information would be prepared and shared in a way so that all caregivers are informed.

During the VSED process the patient may need to be gently reminded that fluid intake would be against their previously-stated wishes.

If a patient with sufficient DMC still requests rehydration, this should be acknowledged by both patient and caregivers as a postponement of VSED.

If the patient indicates a wish to drink later in the process—when they clearly lack DMC—the same palliative measures used previously can be employed. If these are not sufficient to calm the patient, very small amounts of fluid can be offered, along with medication for anxiety or pain. This usually allows the patient to settle and sleep. Severe, agitated delirium is rare but very distressing for all involved and may necessitate consideration of proportionate palliative sedation. If a surrogate decision-maker is convinced that the patient would now stop VSED if they had DMC, rehydration should be provided. If the patient then regains capacity, the goals of care should be readdressed.

Not providing hydration when requested requires certainty that the patient lacks sufficient DMC. The risk of honoring repeated requests for hydration is prolonging the VSED process for a patient who may then choose to reinstitute it, while the risk of not honoring them is denying a patient something to which they have every right. Choices about these relative risks should be considered by patient, caregivers, and clinical team prior to the start of VSED (see "Family, social, religious, spiritual, and caregiving considerations").

When VSED Has Occurred

Death Certificate

The death certificate should be completed by indicating that death occurred naturally and that the immediate cause was dehydration. The primary serious illness(es) causing the patient to pursue VSED should be listed as contributing co-morbidities.

Bereavement of Family and Caregivers

Because VSED results in a planned death, bereavement may have different characteristics than in other circumstances.14-17 Use of hospice and community bereavement resources is recommended.

Clinical Staff Support

Professional caregivers and hospice personnel should be offered comprehensive guidance and support before, during, and after their work with a patient who pursues VSED. Professionals of all types may benefit from support that incorporates an understanding of VSED's particular characteristics.

Disclosures and Acknowledgments

These guidelines did not receive any specific grant from funding agencies in the public, commercial, or not-for-profit sectors.

The authors declare no conflicts of interest. The authors wish to thank Douglas Diekema, David A. Gruenewald, Robert K. Horowitz, Robb Miller, Thaddeus M. Pope, Victor Sandler, and Tyler Tate for their thoughtful feedback on earlier drafts of these guidelines.

References

1. Dykes L. Voluntarily stopping eating and drinking—lack of guidance is failing patients and clinicians. BMJ 2022;379:2621.

2. KNMG Royal Dutch Medical Association and V&VN Dutch Nurses Association. Caring for people who consciously choose not to eat and drink so as to hasten the end of life. Utrecht, The Netherlands: KNMG Publications; 2014.

3. Quill TE, Menzel PT, Pope TM, Schwarz JK, eds. Voluntarily stopping eating and drinking: a compassionate, widely available option for hastening death, New York: Oxford University Press; 2021.

4. Wax JW, An AW, Kosier N, Quill TE. Voluntary stopping eating and drinking. J Am Geriatr Soc 2018;66:441–445.

5. Pope TM, West A. Legal briefing: voluntarily stopping eating and drinking. J Clin Ethics 2014;25:68–80. Spring.

6. Quill TE, Ganzini L, Truog RD, Pope TM. Voluntarily stopping eating and drinking among patients with serious advanced illness-clinical, ethical, and legal aspects. JAMA Intern Med 2018;178:123–127.

7. Bolt EE, Hagens M, Willems D, Onwuteaka-Phipsen BD. Primary care patients hastening death by voluntary stopping eating and drinking. Ann of Fam Med 2015;13:421–428.

8. Schwarz J. Exploring the option of voluntarily stopping eating and drinking within the context of a suffering patient's request for a hastened death. J Palliat Med 2007;10:1288– 1297.

9. Schwarz JK. Sarah's second attempt to stop eating and drinking: success at last. Narrat Inq Bioeth 2016;6:99–101. https://doi.org/10.1353/nib.2016.0022.

10. Gruenewald DA. Voluntarily stopping eating and drinking: a practical approach for long-term care facilities. J Palliat Med 2018;21:1214–1220. https://doi.org/10.1089/ jpm.2018.0100.

11. Chabot B. Taking control of your death by stopping eating and drinking. Amsterdam: Foundation Dignified Dying, 2014.

12. Lowers J, Hughes S, Preston NJ. Overview of voluntary stopping eating and drinking to hasten death. Ann Palliat Med 2021;10:3611–3616 http://dx.doi.org/10.21037/a.

13. Horowitz R, Sussman B, Quill T. VSED narratives: exploring complexity. Narrat Inq in Bioethics 2016;6:115–120.

14. Shurer J, Buchbinder M, Brown N. Emotional, logistical and ethical aspects of voluntarily stopping eating and drinking in patients with movement disorders. Mov Disord 2021;36 (Suppl 1).

15. Keppel-Eichlinger J, Stangl S, Mayer H, Fringer A. Family caregivers' advocacy in voluntary stopping of eating and drinking: a holistic multiple case study. Nurse Open 2022;9:624–636.

16. Lowers J. Experiences of caregivers who support a patient who elects voluntarily stopping eating and drinking (VSED) to hasten death. J Palliat Med 2021;24:376–381. 1089/ jpm.2020.0223.

17. Starks H, Back AL, Pearlman RA, et al. Family member involvement in hastened death. Death Stud 2007;31:105–130.

Poems

As poet Colleen Brooks says in her poem "Rhythm," "Poetry is like a doula or a midwife for me. It comforts me, encourages me, instructs me, and supports me."

May this selection of poems bring you and your loved ones comfort.

End of Days

Almost always with cats, the end
comes creeping over the two of you—
she stops eating, his back legs
no longer support him, she leans
to your hand and purrs but cannot
rise—sometimes a whimper of pain
although they are stoic. They see
death clearly through hooded eyes.
Then there is the long weepy
trip to the vets, the carrier no
longer necessary, the last time
in your lap. The injection is quick.
Simply they stop breathing
in your arms. You bring them
home to bury in the flower garden,
planting a bush over a deep grave.
That is how I would like to cease,
held in a lover's arms and quickly
fading to black like an old fashioned
movie embrace. I hate the white
silent scream of hospitals, the whine
of pain like air conditioning's hum.
I want to click the off switch.
And if I can no longer choose
I want someone who loves me
there, not a doctor with forty patients
and his morality to keep me sort
of, kind of alive or sort of undead.
Why are we more rational and kinder
to our pets than with ourselves or our
parents? Death is not the worst
thing; denying it can be.

~ Marge Piercy

Be here in this world

In ceremony and ritual,
song and verse, stories and tears,
we gently open our hands
to let you go.

We, still tied to this world,
where days are measured in hours without you,
feel your spirit slip out over a far horizon,
where we cannot yet follow.

Deep in myth and mystery,
we stack our memories into
piles of joy and sorrow
as you move from time into sacred time.

~ Marie Eaton

Rhythm

There is a rhythm to this grief,
a rhythm of its own.
Not directed or controlled by me.
It's like the tides or the weather.
Like birth and death.
It has its own time.
It feels so often like labor pains.
Maybe every day we are giving birth to something new,
a new part of us.
Poetry is like a doula
or a midwife for me
It comforts me, encourages me
instructs me, and supports me.
It puts my life in perspective.
I am willing
and I do trust the universe
myself, and all the love in my life.

~ Colleen Brooks

Letting Go

I pray that your letting go
will be as easy
as a leaf falling from a tree.
One breath out, a sigh
and then the long last fall.

I pray that our letting go
will be as easy
as hands opening
to let that leaf gently tumble
into the always running river.

~ Marie Eaton

The earth remembers me

When I die
send me back to the earth
who birthed all life.
Lay my body down.

The earth remembers me.
Cover me with alfalfa,
sweetgrass, flowers and cedar boughs,
I am ready for this new birth.

The microbes in my body and the bacteria
in nature's covering blanket
know how to take me back.
How to transform flesh and bone

into soil to layer into garden beds
or to strew across the forest floor
In yellow leaves and bright moss
near the small lake cradling music.

And in the great cycle, all I have been
will again become *Samsāra** –
part of the continuing loop of life,
death and rebirth at the heart of everything.

*The cycle of life and death.
In Hinduism, the eternal cycle is called Samsāra.

~ Marie Eaton

on my last day

here on Earth
let me be like I
was on my very
first day

let me be
ready for my
great voyage
between worlds

let me be ready
to ride the cosmic
river of the vast unknown

on my last day
here on Earth
let me be like I
was on my very first

let me be
ready to see what
all the fuss is on
the other side of
the womb that I've been
hearing so much about

let me be
ready to be bathed in
a light that I could have
never have imagined

let me be
ready to be held in
the arms by my lovely
creator and to feel safer
than I ever have before

on my last day
here on Earth
let me be like I
was on my very first

let me be
ready to see the smiling faces
of all those who have been
eagerly waiting to meet me

let me be
ready to be swaddled up
in the warmest cotton
blanket of fresh starts

on my last day
here on Earth
let me be like
I was on my very first
covered in the
miracle of creation

no wonder newborn
babies cry
no wonder 45-year old
men cry

it's all such an adventure
it's all such a journey
it's all such a circle
it's all such a flowing river
it's all such an endless passage

it's all such a mystery
and it goes on and on and on
and on and on

it all goes on
and we go on and on and on
and on and on
we all go on

oh, divine light
oh, sacred spirit
oh, God

please let me
go on and on and on
and on and on

oh, I can't wait to see
what comes next

~ john roedel

Laying In

We lay you in and lay you down.
Leaf and bark, grass and bone.
Return your body to holy ground.
All a circle, coming home.

Skin and sinew turn to soil
as you transform to leafy loam.
Dark rich earth, moist and cool.
All a circle, coming home.

We'll spread your spirit beneath the trees
Into the roots of time.
While all the flowers will whisper
Wild wishes into the light.

We lay you in and let you go
to the mystery of all unknown.
The eternal ebb and flow.
All a circle, coming home.

~ Marie Eaton

every night before I go to sleep

I invite all of my beloveds who have died
to join me around my bed to sing with me

when I was younger
the attendance was sparse
it was like a barbershop quartet
of a few deceased loved ones and me
squeaking out a few
sweet improvised tunes
about the miracles of
this life and afterlife
in the echo chamber of
my quieting heart

but now that I'm older
the more crowded my
bedroom is getting
and the louder the singing
has become

lately some of my beloveds
are even bringing their instruments
to play around my bed
it's not a seance
it's a symphony

there are so
many beloveds
showing up to
help me compose
that I've had to ask
them to stand close
to each other

now, at bedtime
my packed bedroom has become
a bustling concert hall
some nights we play
the rock and roll of
gratitude

and some nights we all
hold classical violins and
play songs about
the energy of love
that radiates out
of the beating heart
of the universe

some nights we play the jazz
of how wonderfully terrifying it
can be to give our hearts
to each other

some nights we
sing acapella

some nights
we just hum

it doesn't really matter
what style we choose
to play because with every chord
this community of
beloved ghosts and
I create together
the less afraid of death I become

as it turns out
this adventure we
are on together
is all music
and the beat goes
on and on and on and…

~ john roedel

Reader's Personal Notes and Reflections

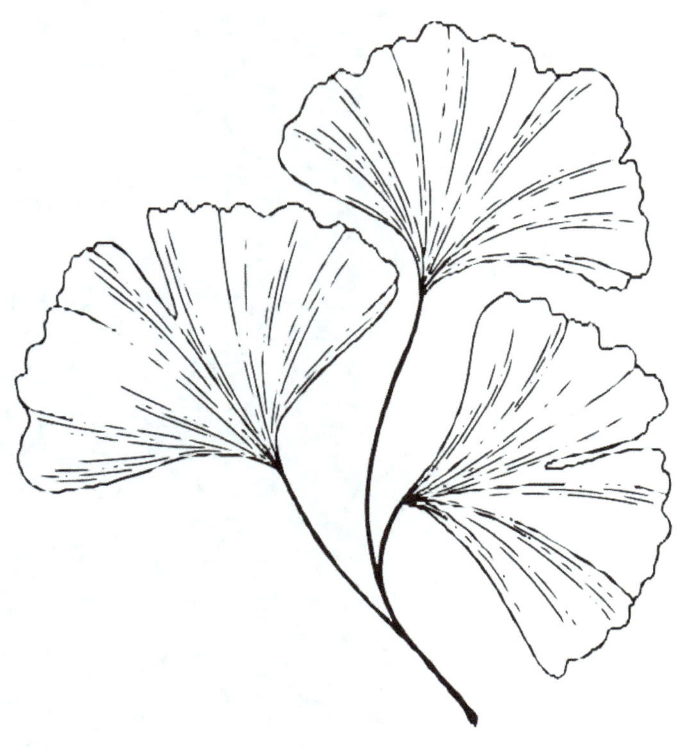

When faced with new information and experiences, humans learn and process our emotions in many different ways. Some of us learn through experience, some by reading or hearing, some by writing or drawing.

As you support your Individual during VSED, use these pages as spaces to note what you are learning and to express your thoughts, feelings and memories. Feel free to jot notes, keep track of your experience, draw pictures, or simply doodle.

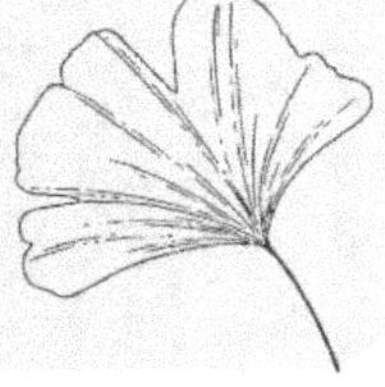

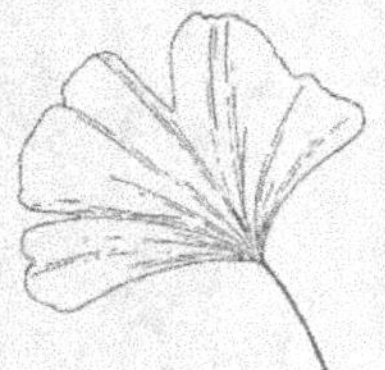

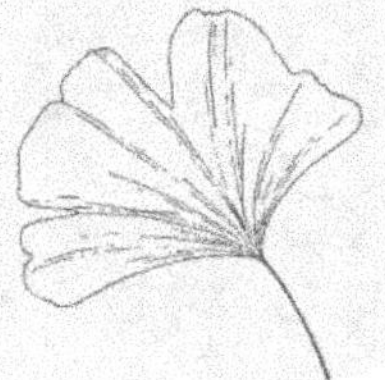

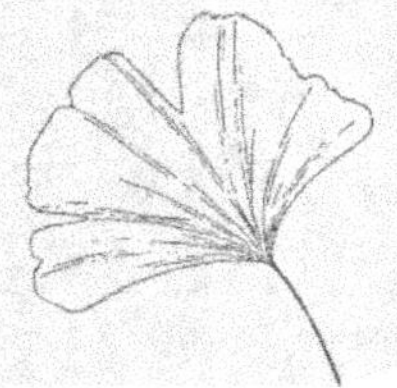

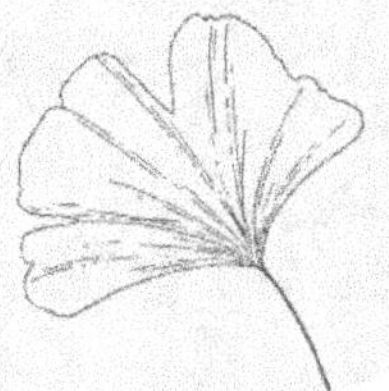